A VERY SIMPLE GARDEN BOOK: VEGETABLES

A *Very* SIMPLE GARDEN BOOK: VEGETABLES

ROHN ENGH

ILLUSTRATIONS BY THE AUTHOR

PAUL S. ERIKSSON

Middlebury • Vermont

CONTENTS

PREFACE

The way Nature does it, a seed falls to the ground, it's nourished by rain and sun, and presto! you have a vegetable. That's simple enough. . .unless a few variables are thrown in . . .like a bird comes along and gobbles up the seed, or the sun dries it out, no rain falls, someone or something steps on the plant, a frost kills the blossom, an insect eats the leaves off it, or a woodland creature comes along and eats the final product.

When man invented the art of gardening (or was it a woman?), he (she) began building a huge superstructure of technical techniques to combat most of the variables mentioned above. As technology progressed, so did gardening techniques — to a point where much of the creativeness and joy of gardening have been lost in lieu of a mountain of horticultural information crammed into instructional tomes. The beginning gardener needs an instruction book to read the instruction books.

But what if you wanted to fly, and the aeronautical instructor sat you at the controls of a 747 and began instructing and you said, "But I wanted to spend my time flying, not learning all this. Don't you have something simpler, like gliding?"

This, then, is a book about gliding in the garden, and it's dedicated to all those garden pilots who wish simply to glide through their first gardens. 747's can wait.

I wish to thank my wife, Gerry, who, along with rain, sun, and soil, helps my plants grow. She also helped this book grow!. . .and Cliff Gorka and Cathy Dorau, two fellow gardeners, for their generous help in passing judgment on the contents.

ROHN ENGH

Star Prairie, Wisconsin, 1977

A VERY SIMPLE GARDEN BOOK: VEGETABLES

THE
TASTE-OF-GARDEN

•

From my office window, looking out on Main Street in Star Prairie, Wisconsin, I look across to Bob's Market. I'm the editor and publisher of the weekly, *Apple River Journal*. Bob's Market is our local grocery store, and the place where townspeople do their trading.

In the summertime and fall, very few local people are buying vegetables. Instead, they're comparing notes when they meet.

"Your tomatoes ripe yet?"

"We got our first dozen corn last night."

"We canned 25 jars of pickles over the weekend."

Star Prairie is a village of 422 and everyone in town learns gardening by osmosis. Having a home out here without a garden is like having a truck without tires.

If a garden problem arises, they talk it over with friends and come up with a variety of ways to solve it.

But how does the person who lives far removed from a country hamlet learn about gardening? The beginner — how does he start from scratch?

The information on the back of seed packets isn't enough. The would-be gardener usually finds himself or herself in the local library, staring in awe at the thick volumes on gardening.

True gardeners eat, sleep, and think Garden. And people who write about gardening are no less guilty — they love to expound on and on. Books on the subject are usually written by the "experts" and seemingly *for* the experts. But who needs to know so much about gardening all at once? Who, in fact, can filter out of the average garden manual the 1-2-3 steps that lead to enjoying the taste of a few hearty home-grown vegetables on the table?

As you look longingly at that available garden space in your yard, have you ever wanted to know, in plain language, how to have it produce succulent, fresh, wholesome vegetables — the kind that taste better and cost less than those from *ye olde* super market?

Some time ago, before we moved to Star Prairie, to a farm just outside of town, we were living in suburbia. I got the urge to spade up the backyard and drop in a few seeds.

I dropped into our local library to get some expert advice. The librarian referred me to the agriculture section. There was no "simple" garden book available. I suffered through the heavy agricultural tomes, vowing someday to write a short, simple how-to for very green beginners like myself.

I took notes that first year. I asked myself questions so simple (yet so immediately important) that when I look back on them today, I find myself laughing out loud! No wonder garden experts find it hard to explain the rudiments of gardening to a beginner.

For example, most garden books never let you know the size a vegetable should be when you harvest it.

To the expert gardener that question might sound preposterous. But to the beginner who doesn't know that a radish will get "woody" or broccoli will go to seed if not harvested early enough, that information is vital.

Here is a simple garden book, divided into three main sections, according to the garden size you may want to bite into:

Section 1: The Taste of Garden

Section 2: The Plateful of Garden

Section 3: The Garden Smörgasbord

The first section is for those who may want to go slow at first and plant uncomplicated things like beans, tomatoes, carrots, and lettuce. It's for those who don't want to be bothered at this stage with trimming Brussels sprouts or snipping melon buds. You'll want to spare just enough attention to your first "Taste of Garden" to make sure the carrots get loving weeding care and the beans are harvested at the right snapping time.

If, on the other hand, you want to jump into this with both feet and set out a good-sized garden, or maybe graduate to something like this in your second season, then Section Two, the "Plateful," is for you.

And for the intrepid, the third section, the "smorgasbord garden," launches into the how-to's of setting an extensive garden into motion and maturity.

Whichever garden size fits you, you will find I have kept my promise and kept this. . .a very simple garden book.

•

How would you like to serve fresh salad makin's next summer?

> tomatoes
> lettuce
> onions
> radishes
> cucumbers

— all grown on your land, and by you?

They're easy to grow! Give them some sunlight, some water, and some good soil to grow in, and watch them take off.

How would you like to serve fresh green beans to your dinner guests, or surprise them with fresh home-grown carrot slices? They're easy to grow.

And how would you like to display a half-dozen big heads of cabbage to your visitors? Cabbage is fun to grow.

Gardens will grow anywhere grass will grow, and I have seen gardens growing in adventurous places: along the "el" line in Chicago, in suburban Philadelphia backyards, in the mountains behind Denver.

If you are hesitant because you have too many trees in your yard, don't be. The grass grows, doesn't it? Yes, most plants need a certain amount of sunlight, but it needn't always be direct. Pumpkins can grow beneath the corn and consistently produce a good harvest. In direct sun, you'll get six dozen tomatoes. In partial shade, you'll come out with five dozen — okay? It's not worth cutting down a tree for a dozen tomatoes.

A good rule of thumb is: Make sure your garden gets at least six hours of sunlight. With about thirteen hours of sunlight available to you throughout the day, you can surely find a place that gets six.

LOCATING YOUR PATCH

Locate your garden patch in a place in your yard that is both quite sunny and level. Valleys or low spots encourage too much moisture, and slopes cause the water to run off too quickly.

Using some stakes, mark off an area about the size of an average kitchen. You might look at your staked-out spot and

Gardening can be a family affair.

feel it looks too modest, and be tempted to expand. Don't give in, unless you have promises from a lot of helpers for the weeding program later in the summer. Your first-year garden should be small enough to give you a chance to get to know your plants and care for them without undue effort.

If you can, arrange your patch so that your rows run north and south. If they run east and west, there's a chance that larger plants like corn might shade the smaller plants all day.

And, if you view the garden from your window, arrange it so that the tallest vegetables are in the background, and the shortest in front. That way you can admire everything at a glance while you're having your morning coffee.

Mark out your rows with stakes and strings. Make them nice and parallel so that your plant rows will give a pleasant appearance as you watch the garden grow. Let the strings remain, at least for a few weeks, so you'll be able to know which sprouts are your plants and which are the weeds.

Use a string as a guideline.

THE TOOLS

A spade, hoe, rake, trowel, and hand cultivator are all you will need in your first garden. They are available at any hardware store.

If you're a natural-impulse buyer, you'll find several kinds of spades, hoes, and rakes, all of which do a good job. If you're a budget gardener, these are the most versatile: a square-tip garden spade, a steel-bow garden rake, and a straight-edge "onion" hoe.

You might want to look into renting a Rototiller for the day. Many hardware stores have them for rent.

Pick up some garden labels — small, flat sticks that you can write the names of your plants on with indelible ink.

THE SOIL

You've seen a vegetable patch that looks like it's having a struggle to grow? It's most likely suffering not from too little

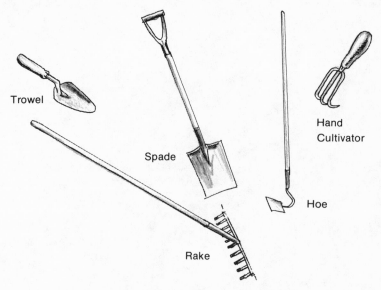

Trowel

Spade

Hand Cultivator

Hoe

Rake

moisture or sunlight, but from lack of good soil.

Unless your home is sitting on virgin soil or rich fertile farmland, your homesite was probably levelled out to sub-soil level, and left only with a thin replacement layer of topsoil for a ground cover. With your garden spade, make a test. Remove the top two or three inches of sod from a three foot square area of your garden patch. How does the soil underneath look?

If it's rich and black like the sod you just dug off, you're in luck. You have excellent soil to work with. This is the stuff that's filled with nutrients. Spade it under and you're ready to plant your first garden.

On the other hand, it's not first-class soil for your garden patch if the soil is gritty, sandy, rocky, or like clay. One remedy is to haul a pick-up load of black dirt to your garden area. But this can be expensive, especially if a pick-up isn't handy.

Here's an easier remedy: consider the subsoil as nothing more than a vehicle for holding the rows of rich soil that will feed your plants. Remove all of the top two or three inches of sod and pile it in one heap. Set up your pegs and strings for your plant rows. (Later on we'll talk about how to space the

Turn your garden soil over with a spade.

rows.) With your spade, dig the subsoil out of your first row to a depth of five inches.

Now break up the sod in your topsoil pile and remove the grass from the dirt. (Just hang onto the grass and shake the dirt off.) Toss away the grass and fill your trench with the black dirt.

Do this for the other rows in your garden patch. Keep the strings intact to make sure you both dig a straight row and plant your seeds in a straight row. If you're generous with filling your five-inch trenches with black dirt, as you should be, you'll probably run out. You can find more at the local nursery, landscaper's, or in the woods.

If you are of a mind to boost the fertilization of your vegetables with chemicals, you might inquire when you visit your nurseryman which all-around fertilizer he might recommend for your garden. Nitrogen, phosphorous, and potash (NKP) are the chemicals he'll be selling you. Generally speaking, nitrogen is for the leaves and stems, phosphorous is for the flowers and fruit, and potash is for the seeds and roots.

Experimentation is fun, and you might want to try some chemical fertilizers on part of your garden to test its worth. Here in Star Prairie, folks find there's enough NKP in ordinary rich dark humus — enough to supply all their garden needs.

Once you get your garden going, you might want to fortify your garden soil with "compost," a natural garden fertilizer. We'll talk about that later.

WHAT TO PLANT

Vegetables "fresh from the garden" are superior to canned and frozen vegetables, but have you figured out why your fresh vegetables will be tastier than the fresh vegetables you buy at the supermarket in the middle of the winter?

One reason is that vegetable varieties grown commercially are chosen on the basis of durability of shelf life and shipping, while home-garden seed varieties feature "taste" as their principle quality. Another reason is that all vegetables begin to deteriorate (ferment) once they are picked. Refrigeration will slow down the fermentation process a lot, but it stands to reason the vegetable you picked for supper in your backyard an hour ago is going to be less "mellow" than the one that has been sitting in the supermarket two days and was grown 500 miles away.

Now that you've decided where you want your garden patch, you're ready to choose which vegetable you'd like to grow. Choosing vegetables for your first garden can easily be likened to stepping into the cafeteria line with a huge appetite.

There's a lot of wisdom in keeping your first garden small. Large gardens have a tendency to get out of control, even for the experienced gardener. A beginner with a large garden could easily find himself wrapped up in watermelon vines and weed pulling when he or she could be spending that time getting to know a handful of vegetables. Certain plants are easier to manage than others. Sweet potatoes, for example, don't do well if the summer temperature ever drops below fifty. Brussels sprouts need pruning.

Here is a good group of plants for the beginner. For the modest "taste-of-garden" plot, try any or all of these favorite easy-to-grow vegetables:

lettuce

radishes

carrots

onions

cabbage

tomatoes

cucumbers

bush beans

PLANTING

In this section you'll find detailed comments on each vegetable. Also, each packet of seeds you plant will have some specific instructions for planting. Make a sketch, once you've digested all these details, and outline just where you want your rows. Since cucumbers grow on vines, you can erect some kind of fence on the edge of your garden. Tomatoes like to bush out. You can tie them to stakes or a tripod once the tomato vines start expanding.

The first five vegetables on the 'What to plant' list are cool-season crops and can be planted early, 'when the buds sprout on the maple trees,' as the saying goes.

The last three — tomatoes, cucumbers, and beans — are warm-season crops and are planted 'when the oak leaves are as big as a squirrel's ear,' (which in Star Prairie is around the first of June).

Many gardeners like to plant strictly according to the directions on the seed packet or the frost map. Other adventurous gardeners like to plant earlier than the recommendations, hoping that no frost will come along and nip their warm weather plants. If they are successful, they will have an earlier harvest, providing the spring has been unseasonably warm. If the spring is cool, however, seeds planted sometimes two weeks later in the season will catch up with those planted early.

If you're curious as to how long it takes your seeds to sprout at different temperatures, make an indoor test when snow is still on the ground. Plant a few of your seeds in an egg carton filled with dirt and place it in a cool part of the house. Plant the same seed in another egg carton and place it in a warm part of the house. Keep both egg cartons well watered. Since seedlings don't get any sunlight in your garden while they're germinating underground, there's no need to set them by a sunny window in your house. This indoor test will not only give you an idea of how soon you can expect your plants to appear, but it'll also aid you in identifying which plants are yours and which are just visiting weeds.

Let's move outdoors and go to work. If you haven't already, check the dampness of your garden soil. If it forms a small ball when you squeeze a handful of it, it's still too damp to begin working up your garden. If it crumbles into fine bits between your thumb and fingers, you're ready to plant your seeds.

Stake each end of the row you are going to plant and draw your string taut and reasonably close to the ground. Make a furrow according to the size of the seed. Small seeds need a shallow furrow which you can draw with your finger or a small stick. Beans need a deeper furrow since these seeds will be covered with a couple of inches of soil. You can use the corner of your hoe to make deeper furrows.

Open the seed packet and pour the fine seed (such as lettuce and radish) into your palm. Drop about four seeds to an inch down the length of the row. You can mix some sand with the seed if you find it too tiny for your fingers. The sand will help to distribute it more evenly. Plant the big seeds one at a time, according to the spacing on the seed packet.

Cover the seeds with soil — the finer the better so that the seedlings won't have to struggle to get through to the surface. Gently tramp down the rows with your shoe or hoe. This forces the moist soil around the seed and prevents the soil and the seed from drying out.

Some seeds are tiny. . .mix them with sand for more even distribution.

Mark your rows to identify the plant and the date you planted them.

We'll talk about planting individual vegetables later on. Some of them, however, you'll want to start as plants rather than seed, since they take longer to mature. Tomato and cabbage plants, for example, are available at your garden store, supermarket, or nursery in plastic containers.

When you are ready to plant them, dig holes about a foot deep and a foot wide and fill the holes with the rich topsoil from your pile, leaving a space near the top for your plant.

Then fill each hole with water and let it soak down. Tap the edge of the container and remove the plants. (They usually come a dozen to a "flat.") Break off an individual plant and with its soil still around it, press the roots firmly in place in the topsoil so there is no hollow under it. Fill the hole with topsoil where it needs it to hold the lower part of the stem firmly and press the soil down. You might have a slight depression around the plant after tramping it down, but this is o.k. It will direct rain toward your plant stem.

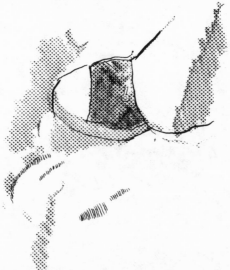

A soft foot helps pack the ground after seeds are planted.

Set your plants out in early morning or late afternoon — not in the hot midday sun. Your plants will probably wilt the first couple of days from the shock of transplanting. Keep them well watered and they'll perk up.

THE CROPS

Lettuce
The crisp head lettuce at the supermarket, with its easy-

to-wash leaves and its eye-appeal to consumers, has minimal
nutritional value. Home-garden lettuce has nearly 100% more
food value, leaf for leaf. If you don't mind trading convenience
for taste, home-grown leaf lettuce can add a new quality to
your salads.

Your seed catalog will show a variety of types. You might
want to experiment with more than one. Your first year, don't
be tempted to try the "heading" variety. It doesn't do well except in special climates or under special conditions. The Butterhead varieties of leaf lettuce such as Bibb, or the looseleaf
or bunching kind such as Grand Rapids or Simpson, have always been popular.

Plant your lettuce seeds early. But not all at once. Every
week, plant some more. You'll have lettuce maturing once a
week. But go easy! Unless you own a cow, don't plant more
than a ten-foot row at a time. A few lettuce seeds go a long
way. . . . . . .

Your lettuce should be ready for the table in a month and
a half. You can pick leaves from it most of the summer — until
the days start getting torrid. Then your lettuce will fade and
give up. But not you. Wait for a week or two, and then plant
more seeds. The rest of your garden will have grown higher
now, giving your young seedlings shade from the hot afternoon sun. By late summer and early fall, you'll be serving
your lettuce again. Or, if you want a constant supply of lettuce, try rigging up some kind of shading device, like a frame
covered with cheesecloth.

Your lettuce seedlings will begin to appear in about a
week. So will the weeds. Which are the weeds and which are
the lettuce? Check the seedling identification on the chart on
page 115. Another way to tell which are your crops and which
are the weeds is to check which leaves are growing in a uniform row under your string and which are haphazard.

When the seedlings are an inch high, eliminate the excess
(since you planted more seeds than you actually needed) by
pulling them out. This is called "thinning" and it gives your
remaining plants some growing room. Save the seedlings you
pull out — they're delicious in salads, too. When the plants are

about two inches high, thin them again to give the remaining plants ample growing room. Lettuce plants need about five inches of growing room. You'll probably be tempted to allow more of your seedlings to survive than is necessary. Don't. As the seedlings grow larger, eliminate the smaller ones. Otherwise, they'll be drinking up the water and nutrients available to your bigger plants.

Depending on the variety, lettuce likes to stretch out. Allow a width of about twelve inches for each row — that is, six inches on either side of the seed row. Lettuce leaves are ready for harvesting any time you are. Pinch off the tender leaves and more will grow in their place.

Head lettuce no doubt gained its popularity when housewives discovered how easy it is to peel off leaves from the compact head. The biggest complaint I've heard about *leaf* lettuce is that it's a nuisance to have to go all the way to the garden for a few leaves when you're ready to make yourself a sandwich.

A lady was in my *Journal* office the other day and explained how she combats that problem. She picks five or six days' worth of leaf lettuce at one picking, washes them all at the same time, and stuffs them into her crisper in the refrigerator. The leaves stay crispy for days.

Radishes
Of all the garden vegetables, radishes will grow the fastest. You can expect them in your salad bowl three weeks after planting them.

The Red Globe variety is a good starter for beginners. But you might want to experiment with the oval and the long white (icicle) varieties.

Like lettuce, the radish likes cool weather. Don't expect to get many radishes if you plant them during hot weather. (They'll have a tendency to 'go to seed' without putting much energy into their radish root.) Since they are ready in about three weeks, plant a few at a time, every week, rather than the whole row. This way you'll always have fresh ones on hand.

Since radishes sprout so quickly, some gardeners like to

plant radish seeds in the rows of slower-sprouting seeds, such as carrots. Before the carrots even appear, the radish seedlings are up, marking the rows. They also help to crack up the surface of the topsoil, allowing the rainfall to seep into the soil where the infant carrot seeds can use the moisture.

Radishes don't take up much room, only about four inches of space on either side of the row — a total row width of eight inches. Thin them so that they will have at least one inch between them. This gives them enough room to grow to full size. If you don't thin your plants, you'll have twice as many radishes, but they'll be half as big.

Start harvesting your radishes whenever they're big enough to bite. If you wait too long, they pass their crisp stage and become "woody."

Carrots

Your carrots will do well if you dig the trench row half again the depth you expect the carrots to grow. For example, if the variety of carrot you plant will be six inches long, dig the trench nine inches deep. Fill it with the topsoil. Carrots need about six inches of space on either side of the row — a total row width of twelve inches.

Of all garden vegetables, carrots will sprout the slowest and even then, not all of the seeds make it. To insure you get a good crop, sow the seeds thickly and about a quarter inch to a half inch deep (they're tiny seeds), and cover with some fine topsoil. If you have some sort of screen, rub the soil through it to cover the carrot seeds. The drier the soil the better.

Keep your seed bed moist and don't get discouraged. It takes about two weeks before carrots come up. Since weeds will come up in about one week, it's essential that you keep your garden twine exactly over your line of carrots so you'll be able to tell the friends from the enemies.

A popular carrot for home gardens is Chantenay. These are ready to eat in about seventy days. Carrot varieties are either short and stubby or long and thin. Choose a variety from the picture on the seed packet that fits your kind of soil.

Most beginning gardeners have poor luck growing carrots because they have either 1) failed to prepare the soil bed with good rich soil, or, 2) failed to thin the carrots to a distance of at least one inch apart.

Carrots can be eaten at any stage of their growth. When you thin your carrots, save the young ones — they're delicious and tender.

By the end of the season, you might have some carrots left over. If you live in a part of the country where winters are

Carrots can remain in the ground during winter if you insulated well with leaves or hay. . .a covering of snow helps. Harvest them any time during the winter.

cold enough to freeze the ground, then you can enjoy carrots all winter long. Here's how we do it in Star Prairie. After the first hard freeze comes (not a nippy frost) we cover our carrots with leaves — about three feet high. In a month or so, the pile settles down to about twelve inches high. We mark our "winter carrot" row with tall stakes so that we'll be able to find it in case snow drifts over the garden. The leaves and snow will act as insulation, and keep the carrots from freezing. During the winter, when we want some fresh carrots, we reach down through the insulation and dig out what we need. We carefully return the insulation, and have tender carrots as long as the supply lasts.

Here's another way to have carrots all winter. If you have a place, such as a root cellar or an abandoned well, that stays around 30 to 35 degrees during the cold spells, you have a natural storage area for carrots. Cut the tops off about an inch from the crown (this prevents them from sprouting in the spring) and put a couple of dozen in a paper bag. Put the bag(s) in a garbage can or similar container, and put the lid on loosely. The carrots will keep 'til spring if it's 1) cold and 2) humid, in your storage place.

Onions

If you like scallions (table onions), the kind you pull from the garden and eat raw, grow them from seed. In the North, start the seeds indoors a couple of months before it's time to start your garden. They grow slowly, and they transplant easily. In the South, start your seeds in the fall, directly in the ground.

For larger onions, for slicing, buy onion sets (tiny bulbs) or onion plants (they look like scallions) from the garden shop. Plant the sets with the tip facing up, about one inch deep and two inches apart in rows that are eight to nine inches apart. Cover the bulbs with soil so that the tip is only ¼-inch into the soil, otherwise your onions may not form large bulbs.

Place onion plants one inch deep and one inch apart in the garden if you expect to use them as table onions, and three to four inches apart if you plan to let them mature into bulbs.

You don't need as deep a trench for onions as you do for carrots. Onion roots are shallow, so if you put topsoil into your onion rows, keep it near the surface. Onions like a lot of water, so if you run into rainless weather, give your onions a good soaking periodically, otherwise they will sometimes form two bulbs or a "split" on the one root.

At mid-summer, flowers will start forming on the tops of your onion leaves. Pinch these off, as they only drain energy from the rest of the plant. The bulb is about as big as it's go-

ing to get when the tops dry up, bend over, and drop to the
ground. When most of your plants have done this, it's time to
harvest them. (Of course you can harvest them anytime previously).

Pull the onions and let them sit on the surface to sun-dry
a couple of days. Next cut the tops off, about an inch from
the bulb. Then bring them to a sheltered porch, garage, or
similar place where they can lie in a single layer where they
can get good ventilation for a couple of weeks. This "curing"
as it's called will prepare the onions well for storage in your
onion bin. If you're going to use the onions within the next
couple of months, there is no need to go through all this curing. Just wash the garden soil off them, let them dry out, and
they're ready.

Cabbage

Since cabbage takes a long time to grow from seed, most
gardeners like to pick up a tray of cabbage plants from the
nursery. The dozen or so plants that come in a tray might be
too many for the size of your garden (when mature, they take
up a diameter of about sixteen inches). One solution is to
plant them all and thin out the weaker plants later on.

A fellow came into the *Journal* office last fall with two
late cabbages and asked me to tell him which one was grown
from seed and which one was grown from a plant. I couldn't
tell the difference. . .which is another way of saying that it's
cheaper to grow your cabbage from seed, especially if you
have an immense garden.

But since most beginning gardeners enjoy the sight of im-
mediate growth in their garden (the cabbage plants from the
nursery are about 5-inches high), we'll assume you're going to
start your cabbage via the plant method. Plant your cabbages
with two feet between rows and two feet between each plant.
Instead of making one long row as you would for lettuce and
carrots, dig a deep hole (at least a foot deep and a foot wide)
every two feet and fill it with your rich topsoil. It's this rich
moist loam your cabbage will thrive on.

Some people like to protect their cabbage plants from the
cabbage maggot by cutting out a piece of tar paper about as
big as a saucer, making a hole in the center, slicing into the

center hole and placing the shield at the base of the cabbage plant.

Cabbage is a popular supper for a variety of bugs. A good method to discourage slugs (slimy little worms that look like quarter moons) is to sprinkle a generous amount of wood ashes at the base of the plant. Cabbage-loving bugs don't seem to like this alkaline reception. The subject of garden pests can become a very complicated one that certainly does not belong in a simple garden book. But, since the insects that love cabbage will also love other plants in your garden, I'll touch upon the subject, lightly and simply.

The biggest pest is probably the cabbage worm butterfly (Pieris rapae), the little white creature that flutters around your cabbage patch. She lays eggs (they're tiny and yellow) on the underneath portion of the leaves. The eggs hatch and out come cabbage worms — small green bugs that gnaw away at the cabbage. The best way to deter a couple of generations of cabbage worms from being born in your garden is to swat cabbage butterflies with a badminton racket or fly swatter. That suggestion might sound a little comical, but one success- ful swat could nip an army of cabbage worms in the bud.

If the worms have already infested your cabbage, they'll vacate quickly if you splash this solution on them which you can mix up in your blender: 1 quart water, 1 teaspoon cayenne pepper (or ground up hot pepper), 1 clove garlic, ½ an onion, 1 tablespoon of liquid dish soap. The soap helps the solution to stick to the leaves.

When I mentioned this mixture to the folks over at Bob's Market, a lady said she got rid of her cabbage worms by dust- ing the underside of the cabbage with ordinary flour in the early morning when dew was still on the leaves. This forms a kind of paste which makes it tough crawling for the worms. By midday, the sun has baked the cabbage worms in the flour and they drop off the plant. You needn't worry about any of these solutions affecting the taste of your plants. The next rainfall usually washes them away.

The nursery will offer early cabbage and late cabbage. Late cabbage forms its head much bigger and much later in the season and is the kind that's good for storing. Early cabbage is better adapted to summer heat and matures earlier. Like with beer, only the experts can detect any difference in taste.

Cabbage needs a lot of sunlight and water. If a maturing cabbage plant is allowed to go with no moisture for a couple of weeks, the head has a tendency to split open. If your cabbage plant doesn't get at least ten hours of sunlight each day, you can expect a smaller plant. But, as we said earlier, it's not worth cutting a shade tree down in your backyard to get forty-five pounds of cabbage instead of thirty.

You can harvest your cabbage just about any time you feel like it. The time to harvest a cabbage is when a member of the family says, "I'd like to taste some of our home-grown cabbage." If you harvest a cabbage that's inferior in size, who's going to know or complain? Especially if you've thrilled them with a tasty ham and cabbage dinner.

If you want to wait 'til the optimum time to harvest your cabbage, do it by the touch method. If the head feels firm, it's ready to harvest. Don't go by "size," since cabbages vary according to variety and weather conditions. Remove the thick outer leaves until you come to the solid inner core of the cabbage head.

If you plant your cabbage from seed (check the seed packet for best time to start), sow either early or late cabbage or both in flats (which you can buy at a garden shop). When they are about four inches high, transplant them to the garden. (In Section Three, we'll talk more about transplanting.)

In keeping my promise to keep this a *very* simple garden book, I won't toss a lot of recipes at you. . .but I can't resist offering this recipe for frozen cabbage salad. I guarantee that once you serve it in the middle of winter, you'll have your guests demanding the recipe.

FROZEN CABBAGE SALAD
Bring to boil and then cool this brine:
½ cup water
1 cup vinegar
2 cups sugar
1 tsp. celery seed

Combine in separate bowl:
1 tsp. salt
1 cabbage, shredded fine
Let stand 1 hour, drain well

Chop very fine:
3 stalks celery
½ green pepper
1 small onion
1 carrot, cut very fine
Mix with drained cabbage and brine.
Freeze. (Makes 5 pints.)

Tomatoes

Here's the favorite of most gardeners. If you don't have time or the space for anything else, at least grow a tomato or two.

Tomatoes grow on a long vine and gardeners have been known to get as many as fifty tomatoes from one plant. Depending on the sunlight, water, and humus available in your soil, you may too. So don't be over-enthusiastic and plant too many plants. Since they take up so much room (3 feet between plants and four feet between rows), you be the judge of how many plants you want to put in your garden.

Your local nurseryman will probably have a choice of tomato varieties available to you. Take his advice. Don't guess as a friend once did on her first garden. She liked the name "cherry" tomatoes and learned in July her tomatoes weren't going to get any larger than. . .cherries.

Planting tomatoes by seed is difficult for the beginner. Since they take 100-plus days to mature, you won't have any tomatoes until fall — and then an early frost might take them. If you start your seeds indoors, you run the risk of the usual hazards of transplanting them.

For the sake of simplicity, start with plants, rather than seeds. Most garden shops sell a dozen plants at a time. This may be too many tomatoes for your first garden. My first suggestion would be to plant two in each spot and decide in a couple of weeks, which plant looks the healthiest. Remove the weaker one, being careful not to disturb the root system of its partner.

This idea, of course, is akin to trying to have your pet chicken for Sunday dinner. No one likes to destroy a thriving plant, even if it is second best. I proposed the dilemma to a gardener friend who came into the *Journal* office the other day and he suggested to use the extra plants as the Pilgrims are reported to have used them — as decorations. They liked the color, but the word then was that the fruit was poisonous. So they pruned the vine, staked it, and enjoyed color outside their cabin during the summer and fall.

Here's how to plant your tomatoes. Dig the 12 inch by 12 inch hole like you did for the cabbages and fill it with that rich topsoil. Press it down until you've got it level with the surrounding ground. If you've got any sand in your area, mix that half and half with your topsoil. Tomatoes love rich, sandy soil.

With your trowel, dig a hole large enough to accommodate the plant.

Tap the tomato plants from the container they came in and break off a section with the soil still around it and set it in the center of the hole. Set it deep enough so that the soil is an inch higher up the stem than previously. Add at least a quart of water. Get it good and soggy. Press additional soil around the base of your plant and level it out.

Since you set the plant about an inch deeper than it was growing in the nursery, this will allow additional roots to grow out from the underground stem and help support the tomato plant. If your garden is shaded a greater part of the day, you're going to need an even larger root system on your tomato plants. If this be the case, before you set your plant in, dig a small trench alongside your original hole. Set the roots in the original hole, then bend the stem carefully into the trench and cover it with soil. Not much of your tomato plant will be above ground to start with, but give it time. In the meantime, the plant is developing a more extensive root system to soak up all those nutrients below ground.

From this point on you can take your choice of two methods to cultivate your tomato plants:

1) if you have a lot of garden room, let nature take its path and let your tomato vine sprawl every which way. In a month or so, you might want to put a bed of straw or thick layer of grass clippings for your tomato vines to sprawl over os that your tomatoes have a nice soft bed to lie on. Otherwise, if they lie directly on the ground, they have more of a chance to pick up a fungus. This won't hurt the tomato or you — it's basically a cosmetic choice. People usually prefer to have their fruits and vegetables free of blemishes.

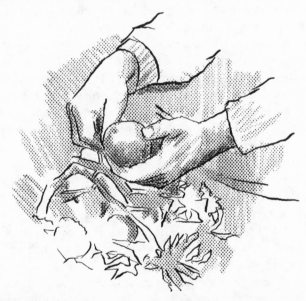

If you come across a blemished tomato, toss it away. Larger ones will replace it.

2) to save space, drive three sturdy stakes into the ground on three sides of your tomato plant. It would be ideal to have your stakes four feet long. (Three feet above the ground and one foot in the ground.)Another support method is to make a tripod of the three stakes and place it over the top of the plant. When your tomato plant starts branching out, tie the branches to the stakes with strips of cloth.

Once again, you and your tomato plant have a variety of

choices open to you, depending on how much time you want to put to your tomatoes. Some folks like to keep their plant well pruned and allow only one main stem to grow. Others allow two main stems. And others don't prune at all. The idea behind pruning is to allow the plant to develop only about half the branch system that it normally would. This means the plant energy will go to producing fewer tomatoes, but bigger ones.

To prune, simply snip off any new growth that doesn't appear to follow the direction of the growth of your main stem. You'll find much of this new growth developing at the fork of two branches. These little growths are called auxiliary buds or "suckers." Pinch them off.

Is pruning a complicated suggestion for a very simple garden book? At first glance it might sound like it. But pruning is like cutting your child's hair. If you make a mistake, you'll never know the difference in two weeks. Your tomato plants just keep growing. And what's nice, they don't talk back.

With your tomatoes staked high off the ground, you have less of a chance of unexpected garden-floor visitors dropping in for lunch. If your tomatoes appear to be attacked by some kind of fungus that leaves them with ugly black spots, remove those tomatoes from the vines and toss them in the disposal or some place away from the garden. Don't fret about the loss. This is a form of pruning. The remaining tomatoes will grow bigger, and, if it's early in the growing season, many other tomatoes will develop on your vine.

This seems as good a time as any to expand on the theme of this book by challenging some old wives' tales that have followed gardening from generation to generation. Earlier in the introduction I mentioned that Bob's Market was an excellent place to pick up hints on better gardening. Well, I didn't mention it's also a place to learn a lot of unsound stuff, too. Here are a couple of examples.

Tradition has told gardeners for generations that they must protect their new tomato plants from cutworms with a paper collar at the base of the stem. In modern times, gardeners use a paper milk carton with the bottom cut out. Like the talisman that keeps evil spirits away — the collar works! The truth is, cutworms don't parachute into your garden overnight, crawl into the soil, and do in all your virgin plants.

Some garden books would have you believe thousands of bugs, beetles, and worms are waiting in hiding on the morning you put your first plant into the soil. TV commercials and newspaper ads want you to believe your garden will look like the Sahara desert unless you dump chemicals constantly on your plants. Trust in nature. For every thousand cutworms, there's one bird, pig, duck, or goose ready to gobble them up. If you spray a chemical on your garden to kill the bad guys, you'll also kill the good guys. Then you *will* have a Sahara desert and the cutworms can move in like an army and take over. In your beginning garden, roll with nature. If you see a suspicious bug, pick him off yourself. For more about controlling insects, see Section Four.

Cutworms are not a threat to your first garden, so don't fool with any "protective measures" of paper collars, etc. There's one chance in a million that a cutworm will attack your garden. He is the larva of the "miller" moth (*Argotis*). His mother lays her eggs in a garden in the fall. They hatch if they aren't gobbled up by the birds in a couple of weeks, and they burrow into the ground and hibernate for the winter. In the spring, they come out on warm evenings (when the birds can't see them) and gnaw at tender garden plants.

It's true that your tomato plants may fall over and die. Such accidents do happen, but we attribute too much intelligence, appetite, and cunning to the lowly cutworm. There are a dozen reasons why a tomato plant may die and one important reason is poor weather conditions. Next time someone says, "The cutworm got my tomato plants," ask them, "Have you ever seen a cutworm?"

Cutworms detest crawling over rough surfaces. As mentioned earlier, sprinkling wood ashes at the base of your plant is helpful. Now that environmental protection laws have come into play, the product from smoke stacks, fly ash, has been found to contain just about all the essential soil nutrients except nitrogen. This might be the perfect stuff to scratch in around the base of your tomato plant. And it may be on the market by now at garden stores, supermarkets, etc.

If you're happy in taking every precautionary measure available to you, then here, for super-safety's sake, is how to put a paper collar around your tomato plants. Take a stiff piece of cardboard such as an index card. Wrap it in a loose circle around the base of your plant, fasten it with a paper clip, sink it into the soil about an inch. Presto! The cutworm won't strike.

Another old wives' tale has to do with shading your plants once you set them out. Some garden books suggest shingles on the south side of the plant, others suggest a bushel basket turned upside down. The shade is supposed to correct the wilting that results when the plant is transplanted to its new home in your garden.

The fact is, shade or no shade, your plant is going to droop over and look sad for about a week and then begin to pick up in spirits. By the second week, it should be healthy-looking and ready to take on the world.

Tomato plants have an amazing will to survive. I can remember once buying my tomato plants from a neighbor boy who was a member of FFA (Future Farmers of America). When he delivered the plants, they looked about as healthy as some dried cinnamon sticks. I didn't want to disappoint the kid so I paid him and stuck them in the garden anyway, that evening. After a week, the leaves had dropped off every one of them, so I bought a dozen more at the garden store, but didn't have time to plant them.

It was a week before I got around to putting the new plants in. When I went to the tomato patch to check out my "cinnamon sticks," I was surprised. Little green leaflets had sprouted on my spindly tomato stems. I gave away my other plants. That summer, I had more tomatoes than ever.

The seeds of tomatoes are tough, too. You'll find little tomato plants starting to sprout up on their own in the garden the following year. These come from seeds that have "wintered over" in your garden, survived the snows and begun growing in the spring. The seeds probably came from a tomato or two left on the garden floor the previous fall. Or they could have been in the droppings of visiting birds. These "volunteer plants," as they're called, are usually too young to produce anything in time before the first frost.

Tomatoes turn into weaklings when a frost comes along. Don't set them in your garden too early in the spring. At the end of the summer, listen for the weather reports. If a frost is predicted, cover your plants at night with a burlap bag, newspapers, blankets, plastic, etc. to protect them. In the morning, remove the protective covering and your plants will be grateful to you. Another frost might not come for another two weeks.

When you're sure a hard freeze will set in for a few days, bring your tomatoes indoors, even though they are still green. The nearly ripe ones can soak up the sun on your window sill. Wrap the other healthy-looking ones in clear plastic wrap or paper towel (newspaper is not a good idea because the ink tends to permeate the taste) and store them in a cool place. This will slow down the ripening process. You can have home-grown tomatoes far into the fall.

If you have more than you can handle, cut the stems out of each one, put them through a blender, skins and all, simmer them for five minutes, and store them in your freezer.

Cucumbers

Here's the vegetable that will have you looking like an expert gardener in just a matter of months.

Cucumbers, of course, are the stuff pickles are made of. How would you like to have a jar of your own home-made pickles on the dinner table by the end of August? Ma Nordstrum brought a pickle recipe into the *Journal* office the other day that she picked up from her grandmother. It's so simple and so easy, the children can make the pickles themselves. But more about that in a few minutes.

Cucumbers are warm-weather plants, so plant your seeds when there's no chance of frost. They love warm soil and will grow twice as fast in warm soil as they will in cool soil. So hold off planting them if it's still chilly, even though the calendar says it ought to be warm outside.

Over the years, a number of different varieties have been developed by the cucumber developers. Basically, there are only two types of cucumbers — the "slicers" which look good on the table, and the "picklers" which are thin-skinned. But they can be interchanged. The difference is only cosmetic. The slicers can be pickled and the picklers can be served in sandwiches and salads — but they don't look as good. . .

Since the cucumber is 95% water (plus a fair amount of vitamins A and C) it is always thirsty. As with the tomato that also drinks a lot of water, plant the seeds in rich, sandy loam. If you have access to some sandy soil, mix it into a hole 12 inches deep by 12 inches wide. Above this hole, plant eight or ten seeds in a circle around the outside perimeter. In a week — give or take a day, depending on the weather — your plants will pop through the surface. When the plants are six inches high, eliminate all but the three strongest ones. Snip them off, lest if you pull them out, you might disturb the root system of a neighboring seedling.

If you can't find any sand and suspect your soil might lean toward the clay side, make a mound of soil on top of your twelve by twelve hole about fifteen inches high. By the middle of summer, your hill will have settled down to about half that high.

Cucumbers planted in this kind of hill, will thrive in the warmer soil. With all that extra air circulation and sun warmth, the soil in your hill will dry out quicker than normal. Make a dent in the top of your hill about as big as your fist. This is where you can sprinkle an extra reservoir of water when you're watering the garden.

If you happen to have some unglazed clay flower pots (any size from four-inch on up will do), press them into the center of your hill and plug up the pot's drainage hole with some sticky clay or something similar. When you fill the pot with water, it will drain slowly out of the hole and the sides of the porous flower pot.

All of these garden tricks are fun to try out and experiment with but are not absolutely necessary. Folks have been growing cucumbers for 3,000 years (it's believed they began in Egypt and Asia) and like the turtle, cucumbers have a way of surviving — come what may. This past summer, we grew two acres of cucumbers at our farm. The first month, June, we had three torrential downpours which washed most of our seeds away. We had to replant. In July, we got zero inches of rain, which — if you would believe the farm manuals — should have caused our cucumbers to shrivel up and say good-bye. They didn't. The result was that they just didn't produce as well. Instead of 600 pounds every three days, we only got 200 pounds.

In your very simple backyard garden, you needn't expect a disaster if you miss a day of weeding, watering or warmth from the sun. Your plants are putting as much effort into surviving as you are in helping them survive. If you can't find sandy soil, clay pots, a trellis for them to climb on, plant the cucumbers anyway. Two cucumbers a day is better than none. And by the way, cucumbers may be warm-weather plants but they don't need sun all day. They do very well in partial shade.

Speaking of trellises, cucumbers are a vine-type plant. They like to crawl every which-a-way. In a small garden, you will want to limit your plants to only three or four, otherwise they'll creep across your carrots, into your lettuce, onions, and radishes and rob them of sunlight.

A fellow was in the *Journal* office last summer and said he had a space problem with his first garden, and solved the cucumber part of it this way. He planted his seeds on the edge row of his garden and trained the vines to grow onto the lawn. When it was grass-clipping time, he folded his cucumber vines back off the lawn, cut the grass and then put his cucumbers back in place. When the vines got just too long and too cumbersome to handle, he gave up and let the grass grow. But it didn't grow very much, since the cucumber leaves shaded most of the sun underneath.

If you use this method, try not to knock any of those pretty yellow blossoms off. That's where the cucumber starts. If you do knock the blossoms off or accidentally snap a vine off, consider it "pruning." Most plants need some pruning anyway.

How do you get cucumbers that are straight and even-

looking instead of twisted and turned? First of all, poor pollination will render odd-shaped cucumbers. Those little bees
that are visiting your garden are working hard to give you ex-
pert-looking cucumbers. Don't discourage their welcome to
your garden or other people's gardens, with insecticides.

The other variables are warmth and water. Even temperatures result in even growth. It's hard to control the weather,
but you can control the water. When our two acres received
no water in the month of July, the growth was consistent because the non-existent water supply (from the sky) was consistent. Conversely, if you water your cucumbers, keep it consistent. Drastic changes from very dry to very wet will result
in drastic shapes in your cucumbers.

How do you protect your cucumbers so that you can harvest them before Mr. Insect does? The cucumber beetles
like your cukes the most. He is black and yellow striped. But
it's doubtful you'll see him in your first year. If you do, just
pick him off by hand. Squash him. If you can't be that vindictive, drop him in a tin can with oil in it. They can swim — but
not in hydrocarbons.

Sprinkling wood ashes at the base of your plant is supposed to discourage him. So is planting marigolds nearby. He
doesn't like the smell, so they say.

You can save a lot of garden space if you grow your cukes
on a trellis or fence of some kind. Design your planting area
so that the seeds are planted in such a way that when the
vines climb, they are facing south. Poultry wiring that is available in hardware stores is probably the handiest. It usually
comes three feet high. If you can find poles or posts high
enough, make your cucumber fence six feet high. Otherwise,
three feet will do, providing you don't overburden your fence
with too many vines. You can figure every successful plant
will take up nine square feet. If your plants are too successful
and crowd out each other, prune them. Snip off unproductive
vines, or excessive vines.

Gardening is like child-raising. Everyone has a viewpoint
on the subject. Depending on the household situation and the
child, most answers to the problems of child rearing are rea-

sonably correct. How often have you said to yourself when
two contradictory bits of advice came your way: "They're
both right. . ."? The same goes for gardening. Give your
plants food, clothing, and shelter — the basics — and they'll
thrive. Anything beyond that is open to personal viewpoint.
Since this is a *very* simple garden book, we are dealing only
with the common-sense basics. If you run into a problem in
your first garden, turn to the best research source you have
available to you — your own common sense.

And now, as promised, we present Ma Nordstrum's time-
tested pickle recipe that will turn your cucumbers into the
talk of the block.

Pickle making can be a long afternoon's effort if you go
about it the usual way. We'll explain the technique(s) in Section Five. But here's a recipe that is as easy to prepare as making a bouillon broth. In the end, you'll have four quart jars of
pickles, ready to serve to guests.

REFRIGERATOR PICKLES
Boil this brine for 3 to 5 minutes:

2 cups sugar
4 cups vinegar
2 tsp. salt
1 tsp. celery seed
½ tsp. curry powder

When cool pour into 4 quart jars into which you've
stuffed as many sliced (lengthwise) cucumbers as you
can. Add a few bits of onion to each jar, depending on
how much you like pickled onions. Put lids on. Put the
jars somewhere in the refrigerator. In a couple of days,
the pickles will be marinated enough so that you can
serve them to your family. They're delicious! If you
wait for a month, they're even better.

Don't throw the brine away. When a jar is empty,
stuff some more sliced cucumbers in there from your
garden.

If you keep your pickles in the refrigerator, they'll
keep just about forever without spoiling.

What more simple way of pickling could you ask for?

Bush Beans

The first thing to remember about beans (string beans, bush beans, pole beans, snap beans, wax beans) is that you harvest them *before* they become beans. In other words, you serve immature beans, you don't wait (like you do with lima beans and peas) until they form in the pod. If you do, you'll be serving tasteless, rubbery shadows of what your beans should be. (If they develop that point, you might as well let them fully mature and dry on the vine to be used as soup beans or baked beans.)

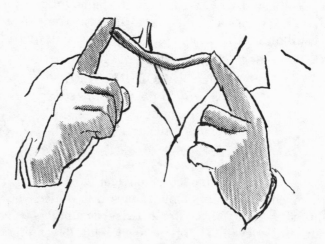

For crisp beans, pick them before the beans form inside the pod.

Beans come in two basic varieties, bush beans and pole beans. I chose bush beans for this initial section because they fruit the quickest and they're easier to grow. There are a variety to bush beans, but four basic kinds: the green snap bean, which also comes in a purple varitey, the yellow (wax) bean, the lima bean, and the soup (dried) bean.

The difference between the yellow and green bean (except for the color) is slight. The yellow bean has a more delicate, milder flavor. The lima bean, of course, is harvested for its bean rather than its edible pod — although there are some varieties of edible-pod limas. The soup beans are harvested when the seed is dry. Some of these are navy beans, and kidney beans.

Which bean to choose? If you are a green bean buyer at the supermarket, you have been serving bush beans, since bush beans are the easiest for the commercial growers to harvest with their combines. But you're in for a taste treat if you have never had fresh cooked beans straight from the garden. But remember this — your beans won't taste as good as the frozen or canned beans unless you harvest them at the right time. Copy the secrets of the commercial grower — they harvest the beans *before* the seeds mature. They wait for the optimum day, pick them, then rush them to the cannery or freezer. If you're planning on beans for supper, don't pick them 'til just before you're ready to cook them.

If for some reason you must pick them earlier in the day, put them in the refrigerator 'til time to prepare supper. Pick only the beans whose seeds are not quite developed. If they're too small, leave them on the plant to grow a little longer. If they're too large and rubbery, pick them anyway and toss them since they're draining energy from your plant. If the beans are left to mature on your plant, the plant will stop bearing completely.

One note of caution. Pick your beans when it's dry outdoors. Beans are subject to a bacterial blight that spreads easily when the plants are wet from rain or dew.

If you'd like to dry your bush beans, you can. Leave the beans on the bush. When they seem reasonably dry, pull up the whole plant, roots and all, and bring them in to a warm place where there's good air circulation. In about a month, on a windy day, take your beans outdoors, put them in the center of an old blanket, wrap them up in the blanket and then stomp on them. This will separate the beans from the dried pods. Open the blanket and with a partner on the other end, snap the blanket. The lighter pods will fly off in the breeze and you'll end up with your shelled beans. Many cookbooks have recipes for delicious baked beans.

Plant your beans in a row. Dig out a trench about four to

five inches deep and fill it with the rich topsoil. Poke holes in the ground about an inch deep and two inches apart. Place an inoculated bean in each hole.

To keep your bean planting very simple, you really don't have to "inoculate" the beans yourself, which means to dust them with a commercial preparation of dried nitrogen-fixing bacteria. The only reason I mention the inoculation is that it is more difficult to grow beans in soil where none have grown before if the beans are not inoculated. Some people tell me they have never inoculated their beans and still have gotten good results, so don't take my suggestion too seriously.

When your seedlings are up and have formed a couple of

Planting beans.

leaves, thin out the weaker plants, leaving one bean plant about every five to seven inches.

In six to eight weeks, your plants will start producing blossoms, and in a couple more weeks, you'll have beans. If you have room in this first garden, plant some more beans, for example, where the lettuce or radishes were growing. Keep planting right up to ten weeks before the expected first frost. Beans don't like cold weather, at either planting or harvesting time.

With so many extra beans available to you, why not freeze some of them?

CARE OF YOUR PLANTS

Weeding

The garden is in and you visit it each day to see if any sprouts have arrived. Nothing. Then, after a few days, green leaflets begin to appear in the garden soil — and *not* where you planted your seeds. These are weeds. Your job: get them out.

And this is what cultivation is all about. With your hoe or hand cultivator you scrape the area near your seed bed. When the weeds are small, cultivation is no task. If you let the weeds grow tall (such as when you're away on vacation for two weeks), their root system is equally as long. You'll have to pull them out by hand. But get at them when they're young. Just running the hoe over them, scraping off their tops, is enough to kill them. They are just as fragile as your plants. Trouble is, their seeds are more plentiful than your seeds. You'll have to cultivate most of the season. Cultivating also helps to break up the soil so that rainfall or water from your garden hose can penetrate. A hard-baked surface will cause the water to run off.

Eliminating the weeds not only helps to make your garden attractive looking, but it keeps them from stealing sunlight, moisture, and nutrients from the soil.

Weeds, of course, are plants too. But we call them weeds because we haven't found a use for them — or we don't care to use them. More about weeds in Section Four.

Another method of preserving moisture in your garden and preventing the weeds from maturing is called "mulching." We'll speak more about this in Section Three. The principle, however, is to place handfuls of hay, straw, pine needles, sawdust, or similar organic matter near the base of your plants and between rows. This thick insulation prevents moisture loss through evaporation and the heavy cover prevents sunlight from getting to the potential weeds underneath.

Of the eight vegetables you have planted in your first garden, only the carrots should present any kind of initial weeding problem. They germinate very slowly. The weeds get a headstart. It's difficult to tell which are the weeds and which are the carrots when the area below the string where you planted your carrots is a solid mass of green.

Examine the sketch of the carrot seedling carefully. Eliminate anything that does not have two *thin* leaves. Later on your carrot will sprout its first real carrot-looking leaf. This will help you to make a more positive identification.

Thinning

When your vegetables grown from seed are sporting a second pair of leaves, this is the time, for most plants, to start thinning them out. Initially, just in case some wouldn't survive, you planted more seeds than you actually needed. Now that your plants have sprouted it's time to make an assessment. Pull one or two seedlings between each sturdy one. This may seem crass vegecide to you, but if you don't thin them, your plants will crowd each other out and, like any living creature, they won't enjoy the crowded conditions.

This thinning operation continues until your plants eventually have the proper distance between each other. Right after a rainfall is always a good time to thin. Your garden soil is moist and the seedlings pull out easily. While you're at it, pull out the neighboring weeds. They'll come out easily, too.

Watering

Your plants will thrive if they get at least one inch of rainfall a week. If they don't, then help them out by bringing the lawn sprinkler to the rescue. Put an empty tin can (a tuna fish can works well) somewhere in your garden. When it fills up to about an inch of sprinkled water or rainfall, your plants are no longer thirsty.

Shallow sprinkling for your plants is not good. The tender roots will have a tendency to grow toward the surface in search of moisture. The closer they are to the surface, the more danger there is of their being dried out by the sun, or cut off when you cultivate.

If you water during the sunny hours, it'll give the tomato and cucumber leaves a chance to dry off. Wet leaves invite mildew on your vine crops.

What if your plants get too much water? Don't worry about it. Unless you've located your garden in a hollow where the rain run-off sits for days, a super-abundant rainfall (like every day for two weeks) won't matter. Your plants will absorb what they need, so will the soil. The rest will evaporate.

Pruning

Each of your plants has a built-in code with this message: *Propagate*. If a wind storm comes along and blows off all the blossoms from your cucumber plant, the plant doesn't curl up and die. Instead, it sends out more blossoms — even more than previously, as if it knew its very existence was being threatened. If a touch football team comes along and makes an end run through your tomato plants, cutting off half the vines, the plant doesn't concede victory. Instead, it produces more vines — even more than before. . .

Now if, for some reason, after the windstorm or the backyard football game the plant is not able to produce more flowers or more vines, an interesting thing will happen. . .the remaining fruits on the plant will grow bigger. The plant seems to know that if it can't produce a lot of fruit (which means a lot of seeds), it will produce *bigger* fruit (which also means a lot of seeds).

Early gardeners noticed this phenomenon (probably when a frost killed all of their blossoms), and discovered that if they controlled the pruning, they could improve the size of their garden produce. For example (all things being genetically equal), a tomato plant left unpruned, would render twenty-five small-sized tomatoes. Pruned, it would render fifteen medium or large-sized tomatoes.

When you prune, you'll find there are four things you'll be pruning: the vines, the leaves, the flowers, or the fruits (or blossoms, which is a fruit in the early stage). This brings something to mind.

A vegetable garden produces not only the "fruits" of the plant. We also harvest for: flowers, leaves, branches, bulbs, and blossoms. For example:

Flowers: Broccoli
Leaves: Spinach
Branches: Rhubarb
Bulbs: Beets
Blossoms: Nasturtiums
Fruits: Tomatoes

When you prune for bigger and more plentiful crops, here are some hints:

Vines — These are actually "branches." If you trim them early, they'll never get far enough to produce any blossoms. As I mentioned in the section on tomatoes, the auxiliary buds or "suckers" are the start of new branches, or vines. Pinch these off, and your plant will send its energy to existing fruit. (You've got to keep pinching.)

Keeping the vines (branches) pruned in this way will result in a "bushier" looking plant. This is handy. Your vegetables (fruit) are all located in one central place.

Flowers — With some vegetables, we eat the flowers, such as broccoli and cauliflower. The latter doesn't lend itself to pruning, but broccoli does. When the plant forms its first central head (flower), snip it off. Other heads will develop at the leaf axils. Harvest the broccoli heads when they're still green (before the yellow shows).

Leaves — Providing the weather is cool, if you keep picking (pruning) your leafy vegetables such as lettuce, spinach, swiss chard, they'll keep sending out more leaves. If you don't pick them, the plant will mature into the final stage of development which is the seed stage. All the energy will go to this development and your plant will wave goodbye to you. This is what's called "goin' to seed."

Fruits — You can prune your plant by taking the fruit off early, as with peppers. At any stage, a pepper is tasty — the sweet ones, of course.

Other fruits have to mature, such as the tomato. . .unless you're making some specialty such as green-tomato relish. If you take an immature fruit off your plant because it is diseased or otherwise damaged, there's no real loss, providing there's sufficient growing season left.

Another way to prune the fruit is to stop it before it even starts, and this is called "nipping it in the bud." The bud, or "blossom," once pollinated, develops into the fruit. By limiting the number of buds, you limit the number of fruit your plant must produce.

Nipping buds is especially important late in the season. Plants are smart, and they don't take chances. They keep producing blossoms right up 'til frost time. But you have to be smarter. The Almanac tells you: You only have twenty days left before frost time. You have *no chance* of getting any mature fruit from that blossom. So, nip it and let the available energy go to the fruit already in progress on your vines or plants.

Here is a brief list of some familiar garden vegetables and fruits you'll want to prune:

Vines and Branches — Tomatoes. Pinch the suckers when you want the plant to stop growing. Keep on pinching.

Rhubarb. Pull the young stalks, but leave some as a lifeline to supply these *perennial* roots with energy.

Cucumbers. Keep picking. Don't let your cukes grow big. The big ones sap the energy from your plant.

Melons and Squash. For bigger melons and squash, snip vines, snip extra blossoms, especially in late summer.

Flowers — Asparagus. Keep cutting up 'til the 4th of July (in the north), mulch well, and let the remainder of your plants grow throughout the season.

Broccoli. Snip the first central flower; the plant will "bush out." Then havest the flowers all season long.

Brussels sprouts. Prune the bottom branches to give the sprouts some sunlight. Start harvesting from the bottom and work up.

Blossoms/Fruits — Strawberries. Run your lawnmower over them in August.

Peas. Pick the pods at maturity. Don't let any remain on past maturity.

Raspberries. Cut the canes that have given fruit.

Beans. Like the peas, pick early, don't let the beans grow

old on the vine. If they do, your plant will stop producing.

Peppers. Pick the small ones for pickling, and more will grow on your plant.

Bulbs and Tubers — Onions. When flowers develop at the top of the plant, snip them off so that the available nutrients go to the bulb, not the seed (in the flowers).

Potatoes. Plant under a mulch and remove the young spuds. Others will grow in their place.

Leaves — Lettuce, Spinach, Swiss Chard, etc. Keep picking the tender leaves.

There are some plants that don't lend themselves to pruning, such as the root crops (beets, carrots, turnips, etc.) and others, like corn and cabbage, that take an entire season to produce their crop.

The following vegetables don't lend themselves to pruning:

> cabbage
> cauliflower
> celery
> corn
> leek
> root crops

Harvest time can vary with different people. We have one fellow here in Star Prairie who doesn't like corn, but loves pickled immature cobs. He prunes his corn, believe it or not. In the old days, the gardeners used to prune the "suckers" (auxiliary buds) from their corn, thinking this would produce bigger ears. But that practice went into disfavor. It appears the extra leaf growth actually supplies more food to the corn stalk and eventually to the cob.

THE PLATEFUL-OF-GARDEN

•

COMPOST

As discussed in Section One, the productivity of many plants can be increased by the addition of topsoil, or loam, to the soil in which they grow. Many other plants, however, are big feeders, and require a lot more nutrients than backyard topsoil can provide.

The best all-around vegetable food is compost. You can make it yourself, but it takes some advance preparation. If the prospect sounds too laborious, too messy, or too odoriferous, you can just resort to chemicals to supplement your soil's needs. However, if you prefer Mother Nature's way of producing plant food, start a compost pile.

At the end of your first garden season, make a pile of all the organic matter you can find in your yard, and the neighbors' yards. This would include: leaves, grass clippings, vines and plants (Choose only the healthy ones; toss the suspicious or diseased ones into the incinerator.) Mix all of these elements in one big pile and run the lawn mower over it several times. Rake up the remains (hopefully you'll have several bushels) into one central pile. Let it sit for a couple of months. Every time it rains, stir it again.

In the meantime, save about one bushelful of organic matter from your table (garbage) in several plastic bags. This would include left-overs, egg shells, coffee grounds, peelings, etc. The peelings and large chunks should be chopped up so that they will break down fast.

At the garden store buy a ten-pound bag of lawn and garden lime. Sprinkle a cupful over your garbage every time you add some more to the plastic bag. This will keep the odor down. You can store your garbage bags in a shed, garage, or garden house to let it mellow.

The question of odor always comes up at this point. When plant life ferments without sufficient oxygen (anaerobically) the "scent" is powerful. Your plastic bag should contain the aroma. If it doesn't, put the whole works in a second plastic bag and seal it.

By the end of two months, your leaf pile will have shrunk somewhat, and now it's time for the *grande mélange*. Mix the mellowed garbage into your leaf pile, and add last-minute ingredients such as wood ashes (a couple of bucketfuls would be fine) and several spadefuls of rich topsoil (a must). If you have some fish, throw them in. Add several more cupfuls of garden lime. If you can find some stable manure (old or new) toss that in too. If your mixture seems dry, add a few quarts of water. Mix the ingredients together and cover with a large sheet of black polyethylene. Over the winter your compost will continue to break down through the anaerobic process.

When spring arrives, the compost will have turned a rich, dark tobacco-like color. The breakdown process isn't quite finished. Uncover it and let it soak up the sunshine and rain. Mix and stir the contents every week or so — right up to the time you're ready to add it to your garden. Wherever planting instructions call for "rich moist loam," this is the stuff to use. It's called compost.

If by chance you don't have a backyard available to you in the winter time, you can shovel your organic *soup du jour* into some large plastic lawn leaf bags, seal them, and store them inside for the winter.

PRE-PLANNING YOUR GARDEN

Now that you've experienced one season of gardening, you know how convenient it is to have a well-designed garden. I visited a beginner's garden last fall and the gardener complained that he wished he had more room for some of the things his family liked: carrots, onions, and beets. But half his garden was filled with the spreading vines of winter squash. "Someone likes squash?" I asked. "Not overly," he said. "But they sure take up a lot of room."

Bush-type squash are available, but even if you have room for sprawling vine plants, take a poll of your family's vegetable favorites. If no one will eat turnips, don't plant them — you'll only have to spend time weeding them.

Just because you have a whole packet of seeds, don't be compelled to plant them all. Save the extras 'til next year. To insure their viability, plant a few of your left-over seeds indoors two weeks before you're ready to plant. If they sprout, most of the carry-overs will also sprout.

Seeds that *probably* won't last a second season are: sweet corn, leek, onion, parsley, and salsify. Most other seeds will last three to seven or eight years or even more if kept in cool, dry conditions.

Graph paper is good stuff to use when you're planning your garden. Each square can represent a foot, or a yard, depending on just what size you want to end up with. Here are some things you'll want to take into consideration:

WINTER STORAGE

If you plan to freeze, dry, can, and/or store a lot of your produce, plant accordingly. Long rows will save you time when you're cultivating. Also, more crops can be planted in the same row, after the first crop has been harvested, providing the distance between the rows is satisfactory for the successive crop.

CULTIVATION

With this in mind, make your spacing between rows so that you can accommodate the method of cultivation you plan to use (hand-hoeing, mulching, rototiller, etc.) The information on each seed packet will let you know the minimum distance between rows that each vegetable requires.

If your plot is on the side of a hill, your rows should run across the slope.

THE PERENNIALS

The plants that come back every year — asparagus, raspberries, strawberries, winter set onions, and rhubarb — should be planted at one end of the garden. Then, if you happen to

bring in some large equipment for plowing or discing, the trac-
tor won't have to dodge your permanent plants.

ROWS

Run your rows north and south if possible and the tall
plants should go on either the west or east side to prevent them
from shading the smaller plants.

EARLY-HARVESTING PLANTS

Locate all of your early-harvesting plants in one spot. The
fast-growing, the early planters, and the quick-maturing, such
as lettuce, onion sets, peas, spinach, early beets, carrots, and
radishes can be grouped together. When you have harvested
them, you'll still have time to plant a second crop of similiar
quick-maturing crops.

When you design your garden, take into consideration the
limitations of your growing season. There's a growing-season
map on page 112 .

The County Agent, whose office is located at your county
seat, will have specific informational literature for you, usually
in mimeograph form, as to when to start planting in your area,
what varieties grow best locally, etc.

THE CROPS

Broccoli

Broccoli is fun to grow. Only a few things are a puzzlement about it and the first is its spelling. I continually misspell
it — so often that as an editor of a country weekly newspaper,
I am ashamed to admit that I have it and eleven other mis-
spelled favorites tacked to the bulletin board above my type-
writer.

Another puzzlement to the beginning gardener is just how
to raise broccoli. In this, a very simple garden book, it might
seem like throwing a curve ball to discuss growing broccoli.
But the vegetable is complicated only when it is not raised
properly from the beginning.

Broccoli, like its relative, cabbage, is most successful when

you start with a plant rather than seed. You can start harvesting in a few weeks. (You can grow broccoli from seed if you
wish, but your first harvest won't be until the fall.) Broccoli
plants are usually available everywhere, in nurseries, supermarkets, and garden shops. They should be selected with care,
as the young plants are almost identical to those of cabbage
and cauliflower.

The roots of a broccoli plant grow just about as deep and
wide as the plant is high and wide — and the plant usually
grows about two feet high and almost as wide. Dig the hole for
your plant accordingly. Fill it with all the rich loam you can
get. If you have any available, this is the place to put that compost you've manufactured.

Start your plants off right by snipping the central blossom.
This is like assassinating the king, because dozens of princes
will pop up to take his place. These young princes will grow
proportionately in size to the amount of nutrients you have
supplied the soil, and other variables such as sun, water, and
temperature.

The bug that loves broccoli the most is the cabbage worm.
These little green worms are hard to see in your green
broccoli heads. When your wife invites a guest for lunch and
serves some fresh broccoli from the garden, it is
disconcerting to find half a worm on a biteful of broccoli. I
have tried to dismiss it with humor ("Ah, but there's more
protein in the worm, my dear, ounce for ounce.") But it
rarely works. The secret is to get the cabbage butterfly before
she lays the egg. As mentioned in Section One, she won't get
to lay many of those little yellow eggs if you swat her with a
badminton racket or similar weapon. One word of caution,
two people swatting cabbage butterflies in a patch at the
same time can lead to misfortune.

When the broccoli starts to produce, cut it off at four or
five inches below the heads, not at the usual garden-book rec-
ommendation of two inches. The stalks are nutritious and have
a special taste, but they are not as tender as the heads, and
consequently need to be cooked longer.

The problem is this: If you cook the heads as long as the stalks, you'll be serving soggy, sorry-looking broccoli. Here's the answer: When preparing to cook it, cut the stalks off, right at the head. Begin cooking them first, and leave them on about three times as long as the heads. Serve them together. They'll both be firm, tender, and cooked just right.

Snip broccoli "flowers" off 4 or 5 inches below bud.

Broccoli likes cool weather. When the weather gets warmer, your plants will start to "bolt," that is, go to seed. Yellow flowers will shoot up; snip these off, and keep snipping 'til the cool weather returns. Your plants will continue to produce in the cool fall weather, even after the frost season arrives. Broccoli is extremely hardy. If you live in the North like I do, you have a taste treat awaiting you in October and November when the hard freezes arrive. Snip off a frosty broccoli head and bite into it, raw. It's a taste all to itself. I liken it to a cross between a spearmint sherbet and a nugget of chopped almonds. But caution! Like green apples, they backfire if you gorge yourself.

Beets

I have never figured out why the good Lord invented beets, unless it was for the annual wine that we make from the two bushels that we harvest every year.

Borsch is a tasty end product of beets — if you've got a sweet tooth — but other than that, I can't imagine why folks bother planting the critters. Ma Nordstrum thinks I'm nuts. She loves the tender young beets and greens, boils the middle-sized, and pickles the granddaddys.

For beets, follow the same planting technique that we talked about for the carrots.

When you begin to thin them out, save the tops (greens), too, and cook together (intact) with the juvenile beets. If this isn't appetizing to you, try frying the greens in some bacon parts with a sprinkling of vinegar thrown in. This gets into the area of soul food. Then again, like pickled beets, you probably have to grow up on the stuff to appreciate it. I contend people grow beets just because they're beautiful. Can you imagine growing the same plant, let alone eating it, if it were, say, brown, in color?

Beets make an excellent wine. For the last dozen years, I have made it in a crock, and I have never as yet had anyone guess that the basic ingredient was beets. ("It's cherry, it's raspberry," etc.)

If you have a crock or plastic pail (don't use any metal) here's the recipe. Before you start, room temperature means about 65 to 70 degrees. Clean means c-l-e-a-n. I once didn't know clean meant c-l-e-a-n. I made ten gallons of rhubarb wine that turned out to be ten gallons of rhubarb vinegar.

BEET WINE

7 lbs. beets	1 whole lemon
3 gallons warm water	2½ lbs. raisins
1 piece of bread	1 cup corn
3 oz. dry yeast	7 lbs. sugar
1 whole orange	

Wash and scrub beets. No need to peel. Cut in small chunks. Put these into clean 5-gallon crock or plastic pail which contains 3 gallons of warm water. Float a piece of bread on top. Bread should be homemade or from bakery, if possible. Cover with something clean such as a tea towel and rubber band. Let sit for four days at room temperature. Strain (you can use cheesecloth). Return strained liquid to crock or plastic pail.

To this strained mixture, add one whole orange (peeled); one lemon (peeled); 2½ pounds of raisins; an ear of corn or a cup of corn; 7 pounds of sugar.

Cover again with clean cover and let sit 30 days at room temperature.

Strain twice. First time with cheesecloth or smiliar strainer. Second time with a milk filter (usually available at a farm store). If a milk filter isn't available, try siphoning liquid off the top, avoiding sediment at bottom of crock. Bottle and cork. In another month, it's ready. In three months, it's even better and in one year, it's unbelievable.

Swiss Chard

I must confess I don't know anything about Swiss Chard. I just haven't gotten around to planting it yet. But Ma Nordstrum tells me I'm missing a lot.

All my neighbors say it lasts all summer long, even during the summer weather. A friend once brought us some in a plastic bag. It kept in the refrigerator three weeks. I know, because I re-discovered it in the fruit drawer. Since I already had ample spinach in the garden, I had forgotten about the Swiss Chard. We boiled it like spinach, and it was tasty. When our spinach gave out when the hot summer weather came along, our friend still had his chard.

Chard is actually from the beet family and although the root is no longer cultivated, as it was during Greek and Roman times, the root is probably the reason Swiss Chard is able to survive the summer heat. Its tentacles extend as far as five feet from the main plant and the tap root goes down at least three and a half feet.

Ma Nordstrum says that the young tender leaves can be served like lettuce, the middle-aged leaves cooked like spinach; and the old, coarse, leaves should be tossed to the chickens.

If you live in a place of mild winters, put a heavy mulch over your Swiss Chard in the winter. Next spring, when you remove it, you'll have your first garden crop of the new season.

Peppers

When we think of peppers, it's usually of the Mexican hot dish — and all those varieties of piquant yellow, red, and green peppers.

The home-garden pepper is nothing like its hot cousins. The 'sweet" pepper or "bell" pepper is a large green variety, a little bigger than an apple at maturity, but it can be picked at any size, and if you wait long enough, it will turn red. This won't make much difference in taste — the redness — so don't fret if you catch the peppers "too late." Some say the sweet peppers which have turned red are actually sweeter in taste.

Buy pepper plants, rather than seed. Like tomatoes, peppers from seed take a long time to mature. Eventually, though, you may want to try planting seeds indoors and transplanting them later to your garden, when weather permits.

I've heard you should never plant peppers next to tomatoes. But I heard it three years after I had already planted peppers next to tomatoes. Out of curiosity, I separated them, and haven't noticed any difference, one way or the other.

Pepper plants have a distinctive quality. Their fruits are exactly the same color as their leaves. This makes the plant full-looking. It also makes it "subtle" in that it doesn't strut around like a tomato plant, showing off its fruit like so many peacock feathers. It is self-contained, unlike the climbing vines of the peas or pole beans. It is, you might say, a quiet plant. If I were to compare the pepper plant to some domestic animal, I would choose the cat.

Pepper plants sometimes don't produce peppers. The reason is simple: they are getting too much nitrogen, which produces leaves, and not enough potash, which produces fruit. Just to make sure you are feeding your pepper plants enough potash, dig some bone meal into the soil when you prepare the initial twelve by twelve-inch hole for your plant. If you have access to the following, a pound of it for a twenty-five-foot row would be excellent: one part rock phosphate, 3 parts green sand, 2 parts wood ashes. Incidentally, a twenty-five-foot row should produce a bushel of peppers.

Pepper plants are not hardy. Don't plant them until after the frost season. If the weather report warns of an impending frost in your area early in the season, cover your young plants with waste baskets, cardboard boxes, etc. Later on, when the plants are mature and sturdy, if frost strikes, cover them with burlap bags or something similar.

Peppers aren't plants you can use all at once, so try freezing them. Simply clean out the seeds, cut them in quarters, freezer-bag them, and put them in your freezer for future use in soups and sauces. If your time is limited, you can also freeze them whole.

Pole Beans

The pole bean is truly a home gardener's product, as no machines have been yet invented to harvest beans from poles. Whatever variety you grow, you can be sure it's distinctive and that its ancestors have never seen the inside of a canning factory.

Pole beans, which may be green or "snap" beans, or string beans, as they used to be called, are long and skinny, just like their bush-bean brothers.

The poles you'll use for beans can be used year after year, so find some substantial ones. If you can't find any, try experimenting by using some tall plants in your garden for support, such as sunflowers, corn, or Jerusalem artichokes. Your beans might not get as much sunlight with this method, so plant a few extra rows if you're a bean-lover.

The bean pole should be six to eight feet high. Set it in the north end of the garden row before you plant your seeds. Plant six to eight seeds in warm weather at the base of the pole. In a couple of weeks, thin the plants down to the three or four best-looking ones. No need to direct the show. The beans will find their way up the pole and in seventy-five to eighty days will be supplying you with tender green beans. If you keep picking pole beans, your plant will keep producing, much longer than bush beans.

Two rules to remember about beans: 1) Harvest them *before* the seeds develop in the pod. 2) Don't work with the beans (cultivating, dusting, harvesting) when the plants are wet. This helps to spread bean "rust."

Once beans start producing, they don't stop. Be prepared to give them away or freeze or can them. The usual procedure is to cut the beans crossways, about bite-size in length; or longwise (french cut). Recent information says that the tip of the bean contains the most protein, so you shouldn't throw it away. We tried it, but after eating tipless beans for so long, we found it difficult to change. We munch on an extra morsel of beef to make up for the lost protein.

Corn

Next to tomatoes, corn is tops in popularity with the do-it-yourself gardener.

First-time corn-planters usually have one of these two problems: They don't have enough corn, or they have too much.

Too much: Corn is only ripe for so long — for example, between day 68 and day 72, corn is at its peak, depending on the variety. There's no sense planting all your corn at once. It'll all be ripe at the same time. Unless you are planning a corn roast, or expect to freeze corn en masse, it is best to "stagger" your corn planting. You can do this two ways: Plant new seeds of the same variety every week, or plant different varieties that mature in different time spans. The maturing times are always listed on your seed packets. Examples of staggering would be to plant North Star, which takes 65 days to mature, Golden Beauty (70 days), and Iochief (84 days), all at the same time. They would have you serving garden-fresh corn for three to four weeks in a row.

Not enough: If your corn doesn't produce, it is probably *not* because some exotic bug has attacked it; more probably it is because your corn has not been pollinated. The pollen forms on the tassels and when a breeze comes along the microscopic grains float through the air and land on the silk of the neighboring cobs. This starts a chain reaction that eventually results in your cobs producing 14 rows of perfectly developed kernels. If your cobs aren't perfectly developed, then your corn was probably poorly pollinated.

You can help by walking down your row of corn and annointing each cob with a sprinkling of pollen from the tassels, but this is shaky business. Instead, let nature work for you. Rather than plant one long row of corn — plant four short rows of the same variety side by side, at the usual thirty inches apart. A cross breeze will be sure to do the job for you. . .

Or if you want to be doubly sure, plant your corn in "hills," as the weathered experts call them, which really means a "circle" when they're talking about corn. The circle should be about the size of a big pie plate. Put about six or seven seeds around the perimeter. When they are a couple of inches high, choose three or four to remain. As the plants grow taller, shovel some compost or rich soil on the base of the plants. This will help feed the shallow root system, and give some ground support. With three or four maturing at such close proximity, you are sure to have well-pollinated cobs every time.

If you plant your corn in rows, the eventual distance between plants should be about fifteen inches, so plant the seeds about 5 inches apart and thin out when the plants are a couple of inches high. As with your lettuce and onions, fill the initial trench with rich loam. For easiest planting, go along the row with a broom handle and poke a one-inch hole (called a drill) in the ground where you want your corn. Corn takes a lot out of the soil, so give it a good meal.

Before the corn gets a couple of inches high, you'll have to do some weeding. Careful you don't mistake your corn shoots for *crab grass* — they look a lot alike. Corn is more circular at the base. The crab grass is flat. The best test though is to pull a couple of corn seedlings intentionally and use them as a guide to what *not* to pull out.

If for some reason a large stretch of corn doesn't appear in one of your rows, transplant some of the thinned seedlings from elsewhere. The transplanting shock will set them back a a few days. See page 108 for more details on transplanting.

Keep some kind of record on your corn such as when you planted it, when it's due, and what kind it is. This information will be helpful in future years when you throw a corn roast in the back yard. You can predict when it will be ready and what variety it will be.

Your nearby garden shop will probably have some suggestions on which corn you ought to plant. Corn is basically white or yellow. The white has long been popular and there are several varieties. The yellow is becoming popular again since it's been discovered that it contains more vitamins and minerals.

If you plant both white and yellow near each other, you can expect some cross pollination — white kernels among the gold. If the kids want to plant some exotic corn such as the colorful Indian corn or pop corn, separate these two as much as possible. And by no means plant them anywhere near your sweet corn.

Harvesting corn is an art, and a lost art at that. Somewhere along the way, the expertise for picking fresh corn was left to the people who run roadside stands. And the people who run roadside stands traditionally relegate the task of picking the corn to their kids, who are left with the decision as to what's saleable and what's not. Corn should be picked *before* the kernels become bulbous. And, of course, if the corn is mushy or rubbery to the bite, you've picked it much, much too late. Or have let it sit too long in a warm place. To discover the right picking time for your corn, make some experiments. When the silk on your corn ears is brown and dry, pull back the husks to get an idea of the kernel size. If you use the same variety each year, you'll soon develop a knack of recognizing the relationship between the fullness of the ear and the color and dryness of the silk.

A common mistake that destroys an otherwise delicious ear of corn is over-boiling. No ear of corn needs to be cooked more than six minutes. If you've been complaining about soggy corn all these years, maybe you've been boiling it too long.

It's traditional to plant some pumpkin seeds in the same row as the corn. You really don't need many seeds, maybe one seed every ten feet. Five or six successful plants can supply the average family's Halloween needs.

When the silk is dark brown, corn is ready to harvest.

For best-tasting corn:

1) Don't wait 'til it's overripe to pick it.

2) For the best taste, have the water boiling before you pick your corn. Corn sugar turns to corn starch from the moment it is picked.

3) When you boil corn, six minutes should be the maximum.

Pumpkins

Pumpkins grow on large, sprawling vines and, as I mentioned a few paragraphs back, they can be grown in your corn rows. However, if you have the space, grow them in their own patch.

There are generally two kinds of pumpkins — those that find themselves glowing on Halloween, and the pumpkin-pie variety. The latter are usually small in size. The Jack-O-Lantern kind grow to the super-large size. Check your seed packet for this kind of information.

More and more people are harvesting pumpkin seeds for their biggest reward in pumpkin growing. The pumpkin seed, ounce for ounce, probably contains the most protein of any plant (including soybeans) in your garden. Here are some comparisons:

	Protein	Calc	Phos	Iron	Vit. A	Vit. C
Spinach (cooked)	3.0	93	51	3.1	8,100	51
Potatoes (baked)	2.6	9	65	.7	—	20
Pumpkin seeds	29.0	51	1,144	11.2	70	0
Soy beans	11.0	73	179	2.7	30	0

(*From:* Composition of Foods USDA,
100 grams, edible portion.)

For a tasty after-school snack, here's how to prepare them.

Wash the seeds in a collander and let them sit overnight in some salty water. Drain. Spread out on cookie sheet and dry in oven at minimum heat for half a day. Store in closed jar in refrigerator.

Pumpkin seeds need to be shelled just like peanuts. (You shell them just before you eat them.) One variety we've found, however, has no husk — you don't need to shell them. And they even taste good raw and unsalted. They're called, maybe appropriately, Lady Godiva.

If you have a blender, you can pulverize your pumpkin seeds, shell and all, and mix this fine "flour" with meat loaf or sprinkle it on breakfast cereal for extra nutrition. Again, store the unused "flour" in the refrigerator, since it contains no preservatives.

Speaking of preservatives, pumpkin seeds have some built-in preservatives if you want to save a few to plant next year. As long as you keep them in a cool, dry place, they'll retain their vitality over the winter. However, if you reverse the conditions (too moist and warm), the seeds will think spring has arrived and begin to sprout.

Save the seeds from your largest Jack-O-Lantern or pie pumpkin, drop in a paper bag, and store for the winter in that cool dry location. Next spring, you won't need to buy pumpkin seeds. (This, of course, won't work for the hybrids such as Lady Godiva, since they're non-regenerating.)

The same storage system will work for your non-hybrid squash varieties also. In fact, pumpkin and squash seeds are so hearty that despite winter conditions, squash and pumpkin seeds left over in your compost pile and those that worked into your soil, will sometimes sprout in the spring. These are called "volunteers." Since they probably will interfere with your garden design (perhaps appearing in the middle of the cabbage patch), they should be eliminated.

If you grow both squash and pumpkin in the same garden, it can be both an advantage and a disadvantage. Because of cross-pollination, the next generation of seeds (the ones you save this winter) will produce some odd-looking squash/pumpkins. On the other hand, you might enjoy the experimentation!

All of this happens because squash are actually pumpkins, or is it the other way around? Botanists are undecided, probably because of the intermarriage. A good home rule is this: If the rind is hard, you can call it a squash. If it's a soft-type rind, call it a pumpkin.

As long as you're in the experimenting mood, here's one: Dig a hole a couple of feet deep and a couple of feet wide and fill it with compost — the richest you can find. Mound it up about a foot off the ground and place an unglazed flower pot in the center. Plug the hole in the bottom loosely with some chewing gum. Plant your jumbo Jack-O-Lantern seeds in a circle (about ten inches out) around the flower pot. Thin them to two or three plants. When the plants begin to vine out, pinch all but one or two blossoms. Keep the flower pot well filled with water all season. You won't have many pumpkins from this hill, but those you do have will be giants!

The squash bug and the squash-vine borer love your pumpkins the most. If you see a sickly looking vine, snip off the unhealthy portion and throw it in the incinerator so that the squash borer doesn't revisit your garden.

The squash bug will crawl around the top of your pumpkin leaves. Look for these guys in the early part of the summer (they're long-legged and grey) before they start laying eggs. Drop them into a can of oil. Or if you're vindictive, treat the squash bug as his name suggests.

When to harvest a pumpkin? They're green most of the summer. In the fall, they'll turn orange. After the first light frost, cut the stems about one inch from the pumpkins. If you're planning on storing them for a couple of months, let them sit in a warm room 70 to 80 degrees for a couple of weeks, then store them in a dry room that stays around 50 to 60 degrees.

You don't have to go through all this if you just want a pumpkin pie. Pick out the early orange ones, cut them open and use the inside rind. A small pumpkin is usually enough for an aveerage-size pie.

Squash

Squash comes in two types: winter squash which has a thick skin, and summer squash which has a thin skin. The summer squash is probably more correctly referred to as a pumpkin.

The colorful photographs on seed packets and garden catalogs will give you the best clue as to what you'll be planting when you begin choosing squash. Because there are so many varieties, you might want to trade some seeds with your neighbors, or if this isn't possible, if you can store your seeds in a cool dry place, you can use only part of each packet and then store them 'til next season. The seeds will last usually up to four years.

Winter squash doesn't mature until the fall so we'll deal with the summer squash first.

Crookneck, which is yellow and has a curved neck, is popular. So is zucchini, which looks like a long cucumber.

Crookneck will be one of the first warm-weather garden vegetables available to you. Harvest them when they're still young and tender. Slice them thin, dip them in egg batter and fry.

Zucchini is delicious if harvested before they grow too large (about three inches in diameter maximum).

Harvest all of your summer squash at the "immature" stage. In maturity, summer squash is tough and tasteless and the seeds are unappetizing. Whether you plan to use the squash or not, pick it off the vine anyway. Otherwise, production falls off when squash is left to grow to maturity.

Here's a recipe that's sure to win over non-zucchini lovers:

GERRY'S ZUCCHINI CASSEROLE
        salad oil
        onion, chopped
        mushrooms
        green peppers, chopped
        zucchini, cut in bite-size pieces
        tomatoes
        tomato sauce or paste
        garlic, oregano. salt, pepper,
        basil, etc. (to taste)

Sauté onion, mushrooms, green pepper in oil. Add zucchini, cook for another 10-15 minutes; add tomatoes, sauce, and spices. Simmer for one hour or longer. Serve over rice or noodles.

Spaghetti squash is gaining in popularity. It's harvestable later on in the summer. Cut in half, remove the seeds and bake in aluminum foil at 350° until tender. When you dig into the yellow meat with a fork, it comes apart in spaghetti-like shreds. The shreds aren't tough and stringy — they'll melt in your mouth.

In early fall, the acorn squash has matured. These are dark green with an orange area. They look something like big acorns. Cut in half, remove seeds, and bake cut side up with center filled with butter and brown sugar, and a piece of foil over top to retain the moisture.

Your acorn squash will keep 'til Christmas at between 50 and 60 degrees. All winter squash keeps best at that temperature. Most farm families around Star Prairie keep their squash in an unheated closet or bedroom (usually under the bed).

Hubbard, buttercup, and butternut have thicker skins, and if not bruised will last almost 'til spring, depending on storage conditions. Winter squash can be served a variety of ways: baked, sautéed, and made into pies, soups, and cupcakes.

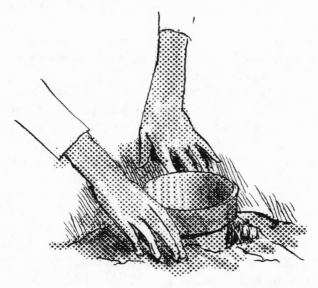

Squash loves water. . .bury an unglazed flower pot in your hill, and water often.

The summer squash generally grows in bush form and the winter on vines. Dig a twelve by twelve inch hole and fill it with compost. Mound the compost about six inches above the ground. On this "hill" plant seven or eight seeds. When they are two inches high, thin them out to the three strongest plants. Squash is a thirsty vegetable. As mentioned earlier, a simple way to make sure it gets enough water is to put an unglazed clay flower pot in the center. Fill the bottom hole loosely with chewing gum. Direct the stream of water into the pot when you are watering your plants.

Winter squash should have six feet between rows and twelve feet between hills. Once the winter squash start "vining" out" they attempt to take over the garden. Direct them to a direction where they won't block sunlight from other row crops (such as toward the lawn). If the vines persist on moving into your row crops, trim the vines with a knife.

By midsummer, the winter squash will have set several fruits. From this point on, remove any further blossoms as these won't have time to develop into mature squash. Available nutrients will then go to fruits already developing on the vine.

The squash vine borer loves to bore its way into your hollow squash vines. He leaves a telltale trail of sawdust-like material. Find him and destroy him (her?).

The first hard frost that comes along will kill your squash plants. Because the leaves are so plentiful, they protect the squash underneath and the first frost generally doesn't harm them. Since another frost might come along soon, that might this time hurt your squash, now is the time to harvest them. Handle with care so as not to bruise them. Store them in a warm room at 70 or 80 degrees for two weeks. This will cause the skins to become even tougher. They'll keep much longer during the winter if you do. Then store them in a room at 50 to 60 degrees. The garden manuals usually say not to store them one atop the other but I've stored them in an empty wardrobe for years that way — with no great harm done. I put the large blue Hubbard on the bottom, then the Buttercup, then the Butternut, then the Acorn, and use them in reverse order. By April or May, we are down to the Hubbard. If a squash has been bruised in handling, it usually decays. Handle with care.

Turnips

Ugh! What tasteless vegetables. Turnips store so well, it would be ideal if they happened to taste like they were worth keeping.

Children refuse to eat them. So do many adults.

I have complained about turnips enough that readers have

come to their rescue and brought turnip recipes to the JOUR-
NAL office. All of them failed the test except perhaps this one:
mash the turnips like potatoes. Instead of mixing in milk —
use cream. Add lots of butter plus salt and pepper. The more
cream you use the better the stuff tastes.

Another man came into the office, not with a recipe, but
with a reprimand. He reminded me if it weren't for the turnip,
I might not be here. Many a Scandinavian, in the olden tymes,
survived a harsh winter by subsisting on turnips. If this be
true, then I salute the turnip. But, with modern storage methods, refrigeration, etc., I predict the turnip will soon become
obsolete.

If you are obdurate enough to try the turnip, keep in mind
that there is a nutritional reward in the greens. The U.S. Dept.
of Agriculture's book, "Composition of Foods," lists them as
just about tops in the green category of vegetables.

Turnips are a cool-season crop, so plant your seeds really
early in the spring, or else at mid-summer so that they mature
in the fall when the weather is cool again. In the South, plant
them so they mature anytime except the summer.

Peas

Peas are another cool-season crop, but their resemblance
to turnips ends there.

Shelling peas is a chore and many gardeners have re-
turned to buying their peas at the supermarket after their garden helpers became disenchanted with the shelling process.

On the other hand, fresh garden peas are so delicious it's
hard to kick the habit. I've known people who will gobble them
up — raw — before they can get them to the kitchen. In case
you'd like to get hooked, here are some pointers.

Plant peas just after the ground thaws or about six weeks
before the last spring frost. They are so hardy, a surprise frost
won't do them in. One lady told me she has good success by
planting a row of peas and a row of lettuce in her garden in the
fall just before the first hard freeze. Depending on snowfall
(insulation) she has crops in her spring garden before any of
her neighbors.

If you live in the South or Southwest, you'll want to plant your peas as a fall crop. An early frost will kill only the blossoms and pods, but not the plants. They'll go on to produce more blossoms and peas.

Peas are vine crops and like to climb. Rig up some poultry wire on a fence similar to your cucumber trellis and plant the peas on either side. Otherwise, let your peas grow on the ground, and spread a thick bed of mulch for them to lie on. You'll get about half the crop. This might make you happy, though, once you've experienced shelling them. Another idea is to plant the "dwarf" variety. They grow about two feet high but their season is shorter than the tall variety.

Your pea plants will continue to produce right up until the hot weather arrives. When they stop producing, pull up the plants and plant something else in their place. Or better still, plant between the rows of peas, a couple of weeks after you've put them in: spinach, lettuce, green onions, radishes, or any small crop which will mature in two months. Since peas mature in fifty to eighty days, these crops will continue on after you've removed the pea plants.

The time to harvest pods is when they just begin to swell in the pod. If you harvest them too soon, they'll be tasty but tiny. If you wait 'til they're too big, they'll have passed the high sweet point and will be headed downhill toward starchiness. Unlike commercial growers who must harvest their peas, ripe and unripe, in one picking, you can choose only those you wish, then return later for successive pickings, and get the most from you pea plot. Commercial growers, by the way, choose their variety on the basis of transportability, hardiness, and color, plus freezing and canning quality. Yours are chosen primarily on the basis of taste.

One variety we haven't mentioned here are the edible pod or "sugar pod peas." They are cooked in their pods like string beans, or they lend themselves well to the Chinese art of sautéing pea pods.

Plant your pea seeds about an inch deep and an inch apart. When they are two inches high, thin them to four inches apart. The dwarf varieties you can thin to three inches apart.

Since they're planted in early spring, they usually get enough rain. If they don't, irrigate them, especially when they're forming pods.

Peas begin to turn to starch as soon as they are harvested. The hotter the weather, the faster they lose their sweetness. Have the pot boiling when you harvest your peas. If that's not practical, cool your peas quickly by putting them in the freezer. Then before they freeze, switch them to the refrigerator. At 30 to 40 degrees, you'll successfully retain your peas' sweetness 'til meal time.

Spinach

Spinach has gotten good public relations over the years. It's rich in several minerals and vitamins. But not the richest... Some of the weeds growing in your garden are actually richer. Here's a comparison. . .

	Protein	Iron	Vit. A	Thiamine	Vit. C
Spinach	3.2	3.1	8,100	.10	51
Green Amaranth	3.5	3.9	6,100	.08	80
Dandelion	2.7	3.1	14,000	.19	35

(*From:* "Composition of Foods," USDA, 100 grams, edible portion.)

What's the appeal of spinach? Garden weeds have never been domesticated to the point where they are convenient to plant, grow, or harvest. Few of them have the taste quality of fresh-cooked spinach. Of course, who's to say spinach wasn't a garden weed also, back in the pre-horticultural era?

The Chinese cultivated this plant and it made its way into Europe during the middle ages.

Spinach is a cool-weather crop. Plant it just as soon as you can get it into the ground. In fact, most varieties won't do well after the temperatures rise above 60 degrees. The plants will bolt or "go to seed." When this happens, it's time to replace the spinach with a row of corn or beans.

Since it should grow only in the cool season, you can help its rapid growth by adding stable manure to your spinach rows, if it is available. Use abundant amounts of compost.

Spinach can also be harvested in the fall, when the weather has turned cool again. To do so, plant your seeds at midsummer. They'll grow well enough in hot weather, but need to mature in cool weather.

Spinach is ready to harvest when the leaves are about six to eight inches high. For best flavor, steam the leaves for about five minutes.

Head Lettuce

Gardening becomes *work* when you attempt to grow head lettuce. If you live in a northern clime like we do here in Star Prairie, Wisconsin, head lettuce will thrive in the spring and in the fall. In the South, wintertime works best.

The trick is to estimate when the lettuce will be "heading," then plant the seeds about three months earlier. Since the growing and "heading" all have to take place in cool weather (75 degrees or cooler), it is probably impossible for you to start your seeds out in the garden, if you live in the North. Start your seeds indoors, or in a cold frame outdoors. The seedlings transplant easily when they're two inches high. Then you can set them two inches apart in their row in the garden. Keep thinning until they are sixteen inches apart. See tips on transplanting on page 108.

If the weather stays cool, the lettuce will head. If it gets above 80 degrees, shade your head lettuce with screens of some kind of nets. This will cool them enough so that they will head.

Another way to get an early start on head lettuce is to sow them in a cold frame about the time of the first frost in the fall. They'll pop up, and when the hard freeze comes, cover them with a generous amount of straw. In the early spring, remove the straw and let them warm up in the sunlight. In a couple of weeks, they'll be ready to transplant to their permanent rows in the garden.

"Head" lettuce is really not a vegetable that lends itself to "simple" gardening. It's actually an invader in this book. Leaf lettuce is so much simpler.

REAPING THE HARVEST

One question many beginning gardeners often ask is "When do I know when my plants are done?"

I used to tell gardeners who were pioneering their first garden season, "Watch the fresh produce section of the super market." But today, that's no longer useful. The corporation farms are growing varieties of tomatoes, for example, that are extremely thick-skinned so that they can be transported easily and last longer on the shelf. They don't taste good, but that doesn't seem to be important to the grocer or the consumer who has never seen a tomato other than the supermarket variety.

Today's "fresh" grocery produce is hardly the model. The difference between a home-grown tomato and a factory-farm tomato is as clear as between a scoop of creamy French vanilla ice cream and it's modern counterpart, ice milk. If you've never tasted real vegetables, then you're in for a treat.

Generally speaking, the time to harvest your vegetables is when they are "ripe". But that can vary.

Being a living entity, a vegetable goes through the same evolution as other living beings. It springs from a seed and bears fruit or flowers which contain more seeds. Somewhere during its life, a part of the plant is harvested. Once you harvest your vegetables, they begin to deteriorate (ferment). The trick is to get them onto the table, into the refrigerator, or into the freezer just as soon as possible.

If you're harvesting the leafy vegetables (lettuce, spinach, etc.) and are not going to be using them immediately, you can retain their fresh-from-the-garden taste by storing them in a "crisper" or plastic bag.

Harvesting cantaoupes can be tricky because they mature at different sizes. In this sense, they are somewhat akin to tomatoes. With cantaloupe, however, it's all done undercover. You can't tell too well from the skin, until you become an expert at it, since cantaloupe changes only slightly in color from green to gray when it is ripe. Most cantaloupe varieties are ripe when their stems begin to separate from the fruit. If the stem seems dry and begins to crack, this is another sign of ripeness. . .the cantaloupe is telling the vine it doesn't need its services any longer.

If your observations fail you and you still pick your cantaloupe either too ripe, or too green, try the "thumping" method. If the melon has a certain "hollowness" to it when you thump it, it'll be ripe. This is a very subjective approach to testtin a cantaloupe's ripeness, but, like listening for a "hollow sound" on tapping a watermelon, it's one that has stood the test of time.

The fun comes when it's harvest time and the kids experience the rewards.

Cantaloupes will ripen a little after they've been picked, but not too much. And they're like watermelon in the respect that if you let them sit for a couple days after picking, they develop more flavor.

After you've experienced a few harvesting seasons with your vegetables, you'll begin to develop an almost intuitive approach to gathering them in. Generally speaking, beginning gardeners wait too long to harvest their vegetables. In keeping with the title of this book, a simple harvesting rule would be: When in doubt, harvest earlier than you think you should.

SECTION THREE

THE GARDEN SMÖRGASBORD

"Man is what he eats" the saying goes. Of the thousands of reportedly edible plants, only a few hundred have been domesticated, and of those only about fifty are popular with human beings. And even of those, only two dozen or so are consistently popular — such as beans, potatoes, and corn. If we are "what we eat," we are truly human beans, potatoes, and corn.

The lack of variety in what we eat is evident at the frozen-food counter or canned-goods section of the supermarket, also at the seed counter. The selection is limited to the easiest, tastiest, and most convenient to prepare. Even in preparing this book, I chose the vegetables along this line, especially in the first section.

As a gardener, though, you can change all this. If there's any truth in the idea that we are "what we eat," then gardening offers something more than a pleasant outdoor activity. You have the opportunity to express more of yourself, to be more of an individual, because you will be growing vegetables of your choice, and varieties that are botanically different from the varieties most commercial farms grow. In a sense, gardening affords you the ticket to be more individual and less part-of-the-crowd.

In this section, I'd like to present just a touch of the many, many other vegetables that are available to you. None of them are really exotic. Many of them are probably already familiar to you. But you'll find I'll be letting you fly more by yourself and not detailing such things as planting, culture and harvesting. The primary reason for this is the observation you've already probably made: after awhile, the rules start repeating themselves. Now's the time to start playing the garden tune by ear.

That's not to say that the new vegetables in this section don't have peculiarities of their own. They do — in fact some of them are rather complicated for simple vegetable gardening.

You might call this section the cut-off point between beginning garden and intermediate.

THE CROPS

Asparagus

Asparagus, in the old days, was a treat only for the chosen few — the people with gardens. Today, commercial freezing technology has made asparagus a favorite in the land.

Asparagus is actually a root stalk and it appears very early in the spring. The root is several inches below the surface and as long as you keep snipping off the tender stalks, it'll keep sending up more. Cut is with a knife, just below the ground surface.

Again, the home-grown variety far surpasses its commercial cousin in taste. The plant is a perennial. Once you go through the labor of planting asparagus, you can sit back and just reap your harvest every year.

The common method of growing asparagus, as in starting fruit trees, has been to buy three-year-old transplants. After the first year, you can expect to harvest some of the crop. But you *can* also start from seed (as you also can with fruit trees). Gardeners who advocate the seed method argue that wild asparagus certainly started that way. One observation a friend made on that subject was, "There'd be a lot more wild asparagus and it'd be a heck of a lot easier to find if the seeds landed in rich loam with large quantities of humus."

Asparagus thrives in rich soil. The popular way to plant it is to dig a long trench about as deep and as wide as your spade. Fill two inches at the bottom with a mixture of well-rotted manure, ground limestone, phosphate rock and compost. Cover it with a layer of compost and set in your transplants, covering them with another layer of sifted compost. As the rootstalk grows that first season, keep filling in the trench with rich soil. This way, you've assured your asparagus plants of an excellent environment. After the first frost, mulch the bed with a heavy layer of straw or leaves.

If you still insist on planting by seed, you have nothing to lose (but time; you won't reap a harvest for five years) if you plant your seed in extra-rich soil. If you don't have such soil, you could transplant your asparagus plants to a place where there is rich soil after one, two, or three years.

The transplants are hardy. I once was carrying a couple of dozen across our pasture and must have dropped one. A month later, despite the almost waterless month we had just experienced, I discovered the plant swaying in the breeze above the pasture grass. It continued to survive for years.

It's necessary to stop cutting your asparagus in mid-summer to let the remaining plants mature so that they can gather nutrients from the air and soil to send down to those roots far below the surface. Asparagus plants, fully grown, look like miniature Christmas trees. In the fall, they turn a lovely yellow. Instead of cutting the dead plants in the fall, bend them over and let them help serve as mulch along with straw or hay.

Lima Beans

They come in both pole and bush variety. If you live in the North, I would suggest you plant the bush limas. The pole type take longer to mature and might not supply you with any beans before the first frost comes along.

If you want dry beans, let your pods mature. In the fall, pull the plants and hang them upside down in a shed or garage or furnace room — someplace where it's reasonably dry. When winter comes, and you have no garden work to occupy you, retrieve your plants and pick the dry beans from the pods while watching TV or visiting with neighbors. Store your dry beans in a jar with a lid on it, and place them in a dry cupboard.

For fresh beans, harvest them from your plants just before the beans begin to swell in the pod. If left too long, the beans become tough and starchy.

Brussels Sprouts

Brussels sprouts are miniature cabbages and they grow on what look like miniature palm trees. Brussels sprouts are a member of the cabbage family so you'll fing their care and handling are much the same as for cabbage and broccoli.

When the tiny "cabbages" begin appearing on the root-stalk, remove some of the lower leaves and stems to get some sunlight onto them. Start picking from the bottom, even though the first ones won't be your best-looking products, which should be fairly firm and full-size. If you let them go beyond maturity, they'll get tough and yellow.

Brussels sprouts transplants are available at garden stores, supermarkets, and nurseries.

Garlic

Garlic is a type of onion, and the two belong to the lily family.

Up here in the North, we plant garlic in the fall in a small bed. When they come up in the spring, we transplant them into a row. If you planted them in a row initially, it would be difficult to tell the sprouts from the weeds. In warmer parts of the country, garlic can be a perennial.

Growing them isn't difficult but finding a use for them is. I've heard they're health-giving, but since garlic sandwiches aren't popular with my normally affectionate mate, I haven't had the opportunity to test their health benefits.

Besides being a wife repellant, garlic is also an insect repellant. I learned this from the lady who wrote to the *Journal*
saying she puts garlic and hot peppers into her blender,
along with liquid dish soap, and serves the mixture to her
cabbage leaves. She reported good success in discouraging
cabbage-butterfly eggs.

The leaves of the cauliflower plant curl around the flower,
causing it to remain white.

Cauliflower

There are no flowers in cauliflower. There aren't even any
blossoms. The center of this cabbage-family plant produces a
compact nugget gardeners have come to call a flower. In most
varieties, the center leaves curl over the top of the 'flower'
and cause blanching effects. If the leaves of your plant don't
quite reach, you can help by placing a piece of aluminum foil
over it, holding it on with a rubber band.

This sounds like a lot of work. Well, the work has only begun. Cauliflower is not a simple garden vegetable. If you want a spring crop, you'll have to hope for cool weather and good moisture for your plants.

If you want a fall crop (you plant from seed for this) you'll have to have cool weather when the heads develop, and again, consistent moisture. In all instances, your cauliflower requires rich soil.

Wrap celery stalks with newspaper and a rubber band.
This will blanch the stalks.

Celery

Celery originally grew in the lowlands, the marshes. If you've got a soggy part of your garden, this is where celery will grow best.

The seeds take a long time to germinate. Start them indoors or buy some plants from the garden shop.

They'll grow about eighteen inches high (just like the ones in the supermarket) but in order to get them to "bunch and blanch" you have to help them out. I've found a good way is to wrap a thick newspaper (folded so it's about five to six inches high) around the base of the celery plant when it's about a foot high. Put a heavy rubber band around the newspaper. The band will cause the stalks to grow straight up, rather than branch out. The newspaper will cause the stalks to "blanch." Don't worry about the newsprint affecting the taste of the celery. The garden elements such as wind, rain, and sun have a diminishing effect on the newsprint. Nothing is lost if you don't do this. Your celery won't be as "chic" looking; it'll be stronger in taste, but will contain more nutrients.

Celery can't stand the cold, but it doesn't mind continuing to thrive in a *cool* cellar when the frosty weather comes. If you have a root cellar, or something similar, pull up the plants, roots and all, and bring them indoors. Set them side by side in about three inches of soil right on your root-cellar floor. (If your cellar floor is cement.) Water them consistently and you can harvest them for the next couple of months.

Celeriac is a cousin to celery. They are both members of the carrot family. The stalks are too strong on celeriac for normal recipes. But the root, which grows about the size and shape of a turnip, has a delicate celery-type flavor.

Potatoes

Everyone is an expert on growing potatoes and there's no reason you shouldn't be also. Potatoes don't grow well in poor or limed soil — that's the first bit of expertise you should master. The second item is that if they get consistent temperature and moisture, they'll grow consistently uniform in shape.

You can control the temperature somewhat by "hilling" or mulching your plants, and the moisture situation is answerable by means of the water faucet.

If you plant your potatoes in the same location you had them in last year, the children of last year's potato bugs might have multiplied in number and become a threat to your new crop. The potato bug (the Colorado potato beetle and its larva) can be controlled by placing the thumb (yours) and the index finger on each side of the body (the potato bug's) and squeezing. If this type of potato bugicide doesn't appeal to you, then several dusting powders are available to you. If you don't care to introduce insecticides into your garden, then check the end of this section for controlling pests naturally.

Potatoes. It's like discovering gold nuggets.

Potatoes grow their seeds two ways. The first is the little-known seed that results when the potato flowers mature. These, if planted, take two seasons to produce potatoes.

The more popular seeding procedure is to plant the "eyes" of potatoes. Plants propagated thus will produce potatoes the first season. The "eye" is the blemish-like mark on a potato. From it grows the sprout when you've stored your potatoes in too warm a place. By the way, never eat the potato sprout; it could prove dangerous to your health, in contrast to most other sprouts. There are several eyes on every potato. When you plant your "seed" potatoes, cut an eye off for each plant you want to grow. If your soil is rich and acidy, there's no need to plant much more than the eye. Here at the farm, we have often found potato plants growing from the *peelings* thrown onto the compost heap.

It's best to buy seed potatoes, since they're grown with that in mind. If you try to use a supermarket potato, you might not have any luck. Many of them are sprayed with a substance that will prevent them from sprouting in your potato bin. In other words, they've been sterilized.

Potatoes, of course, are tubers that grow underground. When a flower appears on your plant above ground, you can start harvesting the potatoes. If you use a garden spade or pitch fork, and your soil is reasonably soft, you can harvest a couple at a time, return the earth to normal and let the rest of the potatoes grow to a larger size while the plant is still flourishing.

If you have an excess of potatoes, put them in a sack and store them in a refrigerator, or root cellar, where it's dark and the constant temperature is between 32 and 38 degrees.

Kohlrabi

Kohlrabi with its long tentacles must have inspired the space-satellite designers. The rule about harvesting plants earlier than you think you should applies especially to kohlrabi. If left to become mature, they become woody.

Kohlrabi is a member of the cabbage clan, so much of what applies to cabbages in planting, culture, and insect protection, applies to kohlrabi.

For a taste treat try this. Harvest a kohlrabi at dinner time. Peel the outside skin like you would an apple, and cut the kohlrabi in pieces like you would an apple. Put the pieces in a small bowl, sprinkle with salt and serve as a before-dinner appetizer.

To assure crisp, tender kohlrabi all summer long, make successive plantings.

Leeks

Here is a member of the onion family that is rarely heard

from in American gardens. But it's not so in French Canada where leeks are popular.

Leeks enjoy all the attributes of the onion, but because of their delicate flavor, lend themselves to some adventurous recipes.

Start your leeks very early in the season in a bed. When they sprout, you'll be able to tell which are the leeks and which are the weeds. When they're three or four inches high, transplant them four inches or so apart in a trench filled with compost or well-rotted manure.

As the plants grow taller, bank the soil around them, right up to the green leaves. This will cause them to blanch. In mild climates, leeks can remain outdoors during the winter. In the North, bring them into your root cellar, next to your celery. The leeks will continue to thrive for a few more months if you keep them moist.

I can't finish talking about leeks without offering a Canadian recipe that will be certain to seal your friendship with those folks to the north.

LEEK CASSEROLE

Grease casserole. At bottom place half a dozen chopped (bite-size) leeks that have been parboiled. Cover with tomato paste, grated cheese, and condiments of your choice. Repeat layers until casserole is filled. Sprinkle with bread crumbs and grated cheese. Bake for one hour at 350° or until leeks are tender.

Watermelons

I've seen some big watermelons grown in this northern climate of Star Prairie, Wisconsin, but it took some ingenuity. The fellow who did it came into the *Journal* office and his triumph intrigued me so, that I went out to his garden to take a look.

He had placed several five-gallon tin pails on the platforms in his watermelon patch. The pails had several holes in the bottoms. When it was time to water the garden, he filled the pails, and over a 24-hour period, the pails leaked out a steady stream of moisture to his watermelon plants. This, combined with a long stretch of sunny weather, produced some massive watermelons.

For regular garden conditions in the North, a smaller variety has been developed. These are just as tasty as the grandaddy from the sunny South.

Parsnips

These plants, you might be surprised to know, produce the first vegetables you'll serve each spring after the snows melt.

It works this way. A lazy gardener, back when the art was first being perfected, discovered if he harvested his parsnips not in the fall, but the following spring, they were sweeter and tastier.

When the days are warm and the nights are still frosty, you can harvest last summer's parsnip efforts.

Parsnips are slow to germinate, like carrots, which means you'll be weeding your rows even before the seedling appears.

Once you harvest several bunches of parsnips, what's next? At our house, the first vegetable of the year from the garden gets a special welcome, but no particularly fancy recipe or condiments (maybe because parsnips have a powerful taste of their own). Gerry either steams and butters them, or slices them thin and sautées them. If there are any left over, I make parsnip wine.

Rhubarb

Here's another perennial, like asparagus, and ought to be planted off in a corner where it won't interrupt the Rototilling flow of traffic in the spring and fall. The corner, of course, ought to be a place of prominence. Rhubarb is a delight to have around. Especially because it is one of the first garden plants to show a sign of life while the snow is still melting.

To encourage rhubarb to come up even faster a neighbor "forces" it by putting cut-off stove pipes around her plants and then piling fresh manure against the metal slides. The added heat is enough to cause rhubarb pie to appear in her household a week earlier than usual.

Rhubarb can be planted from seed but a quicker way is to buy or find some cuttings from an existing root system.

The plant will last as long as you do — if you give it a good home. Before you plant your new roots, dig in a generous amount of well-rotted manure and compost. Replenish this each season with a top dressing of the same in the fall. Whenever you remove stalks for your needs, let the leaves remain in the bed for extra mulch. To keep the plant going, let about one-third of the stalks remain to do the workof sending down nutrients to the rootstalk.

Rhubarb leaves are toxic and shouldn't be eaten by humans or animals.

Rutabaga

Once your spinach, peas, or beets have come through for you, it's time to plant a fall crop of rutabaga, or as some people call it, Swedish turnip. Although they look somewhat like a turnip, their taste is more distinctive, and their flesh color leans toward an orange rather than white.

Rutabaga will store just about the best of any of your garden vegetables. If you plant the seed around July 15th, the crop will be ready about October 15th, or in ninety days. If the weather's cold enough, harvest your rutabaga and store them in a place that remains between 32 and 38 degrees.

I've found that an excellent way to store our rutabaga is to gather dry leaves in the fall — enough to fill a couple of retired suitcases. I stuff the leaves and the rutabagas in the suitcases and stash them away in the corner or the root cellar. We go to the suitcase any time we want a fresh rutabaga, and this lasts right up to April and May. . .depending on how warm it gets down in the root cellar.

SECTION FOUR

SOME GARDEN DESSERTS

MULCHING

Nature's approach to gardening is to flip a coin. Whoever wins the toss, gets to survive. A casual walk through the woods will reveal that nature takes a lackadaisical approach to cultivating its own garden. Trees are expected to prune themselves. Wild flowers are expected to find their own best environment for survival. Young saplings are expected to shoot up tall and skinny if they want to soak up any of that sunlight on the forest roof.

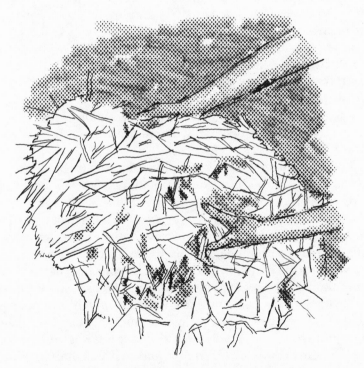

Mulching. . .Use a healthy amount. It settles after awhile.

Nature provides its own fertilization and weeding program too, on a haphazard basis. It's called mulch.

Beneath a pine tree, not many things grow. The pine needles smother them out. In other parts of the forest, the fallen
leaves, plus the lack of sunlight and the proximity of nutrient-
devouring tree roots close to the soil's surface — all contribute
to the weeding program. As the fallen trees themselves decay,
they recycle themselves into the fertilization program.

Mulching in the garden is a sort of controlled duplication
of Nature. Gardeners have learned that judicious mulching
can lead both to less work in the garden and a revitalization
program for their garden's soil.

In general, the most efficient garden mulch appears to be
aged hay. The older the better. Aged hay has several advan-
tages as a mulch for your garden: 1.) It is compact. 2.) The dis-
integration process is already in progress. 3.) Most of the weed
seeds are probably dead. 4.) It's readily available. 5.) It's
cheap because farmers have little use for it. 6.) Hay has plenty
of nutrients to contribute to your soil.

Pine needles and sawdust are also favorites as mulch. So
are shredded leaves and grass clippings.

The forest floor can afford to have a mulch carpet the year
'round, but your garden can't. There are two main reasons for
this.

1.) The warmer your garden soil is, the quicker your garden is going to produce. Mulch insulates the soil, and in the
springtime that means the heat stays out and the cold stays in.

2.) After you first plant your garden, when your seedlings
are only an inch or so high, you'll want to hand-pick the weeds
and cultivate with a hoe. Mulch, by its shaggy texture, gets in
the way at this stage. It gets caught in your hoe, or cultivator.
Or it slips over top of the seedlings and blocks out sunlight.

Probably the best time to introduce mulch into your garden is after the first month. Place it thickly around the base of
your plants and in between rows. Pile it high because it has a
tendency to "compact." In a few weeks, it'll be half as high as
it was the first day you put it down. Also, the thicker it is, the
less likely a chance there will be that weeds will grow up
through it.

Mulch is especially effective for the vine plants: melons,

tomatoes, and cucumbers. With a thick bed of mulch, your tomatoes, for example, can sprawl in all directions without ever
touching the ground. But hold off putting mulch under your
vine plants until late spring, when the ground is thoroughly
warm.

The cool-weather plants such as the cabbage family love
the mulch. One gentleman reports to me regularly on a mulch
garden experiment he is making for all his cabbage, broccoli,
cauliflower, kohlrabi, and Brussels sprouts.

For the past four years, he has followed the same procedure. In the fall, he unloads 15 bales of hay on his cabbage
patch which happens to be the foundation of an old tobacco
shed, which was later used as a pig pen, and now serves as his
cabbage patch. He spreads the hay out so that it's about three
feet high. Over the winter, it settles down to about six inches
high. In early spring, he stakes out his garden with string,
separates the hay and places in his plants every fifteen inches.

His patch is big enough to hold two dozen each of cabbage, broccoli, cauliflower, kohlrabi, and Brussels sprouts.
In a couple of weeks, when his plants are a little bigger, he
checks for weeds, and pulls the mulch a little closer to the
plant. By the fourth week, he brings the mulch right up next
to the base of the plant.

That's it. That's the extent of his cultivation. No weeding.
His plants thrive, especially during the heat of the summer
when the thick blanket of mulch is keeping the soil at a constant cool temperature.

By the end of the season, the mulch has disintegrated and
added to the fertility of the soil. He supplements this with
wood ashes, lime, and well-rotted manure.

One aspect of his system is contrary to what we've learned
about rotating crops. So as not to give garden pests a better
than even chance, most garden books recommend not putting
the same family of vegetables in the same location for at least
two years. But my friend grows his cabbage in the same spot
and he's done it for four years with no outward sign of any
problems. He tells me that he uses most of the pest-control
methods mentioned in our section on cabbages and is espe-

cially strong on keeping the cabbage-butterfly population down to zero by swatting them with a badminton racket which he hangs in a place of honor on an old oak tree next to his garden.

Mulch, however, has been known to encourage mice. If you encounter such creatures in your garden, my first suggestion would be buy or borrow a cat. But don't forget, cats also like birds, which like insects, so the choice is yours.

Mulch also welcomes slugs. The benefits of mulch far outweigh the disadvantages of slugs.

Another drawback of mulch is its price. Most people use hay. Hay prices are higher than they've ever been and farmers are more cautious than ever about letting any spoil. But it happens, and with a little phoning or searching, you might find a source of spoiled hay.

Another source of rich mulch is leaves. The local village or city maintenance crew might be convinced to dump their next load of leaves in your garden, if it's convenient to them.

The mulch system of gardening hasn't enjoyed great success on the American gardening scene probably more for aesthetic reasons than horticultural reasons. Cosmetically, mulch can't compete with the highly manicured look most Americans like to see in their gardens, and their neighbors'. When a strong wind comes up, mulch is known to fly off the premises and land where it's not wanted, such as in the neighbor's lawn. Mulch is also a fire hazard, so it might be a good idea not to let anyone smoke in your garden if you make extensive use of mulch. A non-smoking friend told me about a fire that started in his mulch. He figured the cause must have been a piece of glass that got in his compost, made its way to his mulch garden and on a sunny day, acted as a magnfigying glass.

FLOWERS IN YOUR GARDEN

Flowers are a bonus in your vegetable garden. Flower gardeners don't get any vegetables, but vegetable gardeners get flowers. . . . Your vine crops and other fruits such as raspberries, strawberries, cantaloupe, tomatoes, and eggplant all produce spectacular blossoms. Even the root crops, when they go to seed, offer beautiful displays. Of the onion family, probably the leek seed cluster is the most handsome. But why not introduce "regular" flowers into your garden too? Some have been known actually to be beneficial to vegetable plants. That is, they repel insects. Marigolds are a favorite in this department. Plant a row of them next to your cucumbers and it's said they will chase away the cucumber beetle. I've been doing it for years. Since my cucumbers have never been bothered by cucumber beetles, maybe I can testify that it works. Marigolds are also said to discourage nematodes — microscopic worms that feed on roots.

Nasturtiums repel aphids. They also serve as a vegetable. Break up the young leaves and include them in your salad makings. Nasturtiums, incidentally, don't grow as well in rich soil.

Geraniums are said to turn away Japanese beetles.

Dahlias and gladiolas don't turn away insects, as far as I know, but they certainly attract admirers and add to the pleasantness of gardening. Ma Nordstrum plants a row of each in her garden every year, and when it's time to store the garden tools for the winter, she packs her glad and dahlia bulbs in a box of sand and puts them to rest for the winter in her root cellar.

INSECT CONTROL

Insects have been around for 300 million years; entomologists guess there are about 3 million species, and the total number of individual insects in the world is beyond estimation. It would be safe to guess there are more insects in your county than there are people in the world. Is it any wonder that a few thousand might wander into your garden?

Don't be alarmed if they do. It's a compliment. As they say about the truck stops along the highway — the ones with the most cars parked out front usually serve the best food.

I don't mean to imply that you should open up a cafeteria for the insects, but on the other hand, the presence of insects in your garden doesn't spell doom. It only means you aren't the only one enjoying the harvest.

To get your fair share of garden produce, then, you must control the insects. What is a bad insect and what is a good one? A good one would be one that eats only weeds, or eats other insects which eat your vegetables. Insecticides aren't the answer then, because sprayed without discrimination they kill all insects, both bad and good.

When you go after the bad insects (let's call them pests), you'll be looking for the burrowers (such as corn earworms), the soil pests (cutworms), the sucking insects (aphids) and leaf chewers (Japanese beetles).

Total insect control, short of bulldozing the garden under, is just about impossible. Don't aim for it. But to maintain a reasonable balance. here are some pointers:

Diseased Plants.

Haul them away to the incinerator. Don't let them remain in the garden, or in the compost pile. When you choose plants or seeds select the disease-resistant ones that have been recently developed.

Natural Controls.

Build a bird bath in your garden and watch the increase in the bird population. Here are some of the insect-eaters you hope will visit your garden: chickadees, nuthatches, robins, bluebirds, wrens, waxwings, warblers and orioles.

Here are some other friends: frogs, toads, snakes, salamanders, lizards, ducks and chickens.

The birds, fowl and reptiles also eat the good insects, too, so you have to take your chances. The good insects (because they eat the bad ones) are ladybugs, praying mantises, lacewings, and trichogramma wasps. If you don't have any of these already living in your garden, it's possible to buy a boxful and try them out. Garden magazines often advertise them.

One-By-One Method

If you see a pest, pick him (or her) off the plant immediately. If you're on a bug-pickin' spree, carry along a jar or can half-filled with oil to drop them into. A one-inch paint brush is a handy weapon. Brush the mealy bugs and scale insects into your can or onto the ground. Washing them off with a spray from the hose helps too. They rarely make it back to where you found them.

Early Bird Tactics

Work hardest at the early stage of your garden. Get to know the enemy. Look for chewed up leaves, puncture holes, excrements, cast-off skins, tiny eggs — all clues that you are losing control. By catching the culprits early, you can destroy pests that would have gone on to lay thousands of eggs in your garden. . .

Sprays, Dusts, and Toxic Materials

If you resort to these, be sure to aim them at just the plant you suspect needs it.

Two popular natural insecticides which are said not to be dangerous to humans are pyrethrum and rotenone. These, along with chemical sprays, are available at most nurseries and garden stores.

If you'd like to try some home-grown bug chasers, try this recipe. Into a blender, put equal amounts of water with any or all of these plants: garlic, marigold, onion and hot pepper. Strain, mix 10 to 1 with water, and use in your spray gun. Or if you'd like to apply a thick solution by hand, mix it with some soap flakes into a fluffy lather.

Poisons In Your Garden

Did you know green potatoes are poisonous? You've probably never seen a green one if this is your first attempt at growing potatoes. Supermarket potatoes are all grown and graded to prevent greened potatoes from reaching you.

Greened potatoes are not to be confused with "new" potatoes, which are young potatoes and totally delicious.

Greened potatoes result when sunlight reaches your potatoes when they are not covered with enough soil or mulch. Remedy this by keeping a constant vigil on your potato rows. If a greened potato does happen to come up in your bin, you can still use the potato, but cut away the greened part thoroughly.

Sprinkle your own concoction for pest control.

What will happen if you eat a greened potato? Well, if you eat a sufficient amount of them, or even the sprouts, a variety of things can befall you: stomach ache, lower temperature, paralysis, dilated pupils, vomiting, diarrhea, shock, circulatory, and respiratory depression, loss of sensation, and death.

Potatoes are a member of the nightshade family — and that plant has been known to kill horses. The stuff that does the damage is a glycoalkaloid called solanine. Small amounts can be deadly, especially to children. I've never heard of a person dying of solanine poisoning, but again, not that many people have been growing their own vegetables in recent years.

In the past, we have been protected from unsuspecting poisons in the garden because our food supply has reached us through a foolproof commercial marketing system. If we elect to grow our own, we also take on the responsibility of searching out the minus side of the adventure.

You're probably saying, My gawd, I've read this far and didn't realize I was playing with fire! You probably aren't, since common-sense thinking will rule out most of the hazards. The vital thing to watch out for is experimentation on the part of the kids.

Here are some general rules you'll want to keep:

1. Don't let infants play with bulbs and seeds. Store them where they can't find them.

2. Don't let kids suck nectar from flowers or make "tea" from leaves, such as tomato or rhubarb leaves.

3. Don't rely on pets, birds, or squirrels to indicate non-poisonous plants.

4. Don't assume heating or cooking is always going to destroy a toxic substance in a suspected plant.

Your garden is certainly not going to produce any poisonous hemlock. . .so you needn't anticipate going the regal way of Socrates. But you should be aware of a handful of potentially poisonous items.

Here are some things to look out for in your friendly garden:

The *roots* of the *mustard family* can cause vomiting and diarrhea in children if they happen to eat a good amount of them. The mustard family includes all of these: mustard, kale, cabbage, Brussels sprouts, cauliflower, broccoli, rutabaga, turnip, radish, cress, and horseradish.

The *castor bean* usually isn't much of a bean to grow in the garden. It's grown more as an ornamental in the yard. One to three seeds can be fatal to a child. If an adult happened to eat half a dozen, he would die too.

Ground cherry, Jerusalem cherry, Chinese lantern, straw-berry tomato — different names for one plant. The leaves and unripe fruit are poisonous.

The friendly *rhubarb* is not so friendly if the leaves are eaten. Eat only the stalks. The leaves can cause stomach pains, nausea, vomiting, weakness, difficulty of breathing, burning of the mouth or throat, internal bleeding, coma, and possibly death. The poisonous substance in the leaves is said to be a soluble oxalate, but the botanists aren't sure. It wasn't generally realized that rhubarb leaves were toxic until World War I. At the time, since food was scarce, a government pamphlet in England suggested gardeners could help the war effort by eating the leaves as well as the stock. The pamphlet didn't say whose war effort it was interested in helping. Several Englishmen died.

Tomato. This familiar plant was thought to be poisonous by the early settlers and they grew it only for its ornamental value. Tomato leaves *are* poisonous and children have developed severe reactions from making "tea" from them. Cattle have been known to die from tomato vines (garden cleanings) when they were tossed over the garden fence into the pasture.

Enthusiasm for gardening shouldn't be dampened by information about poisoning. There are basically only three items that could present a posion problem to a normal everyday gardener:

    1.) Rhubarb leaves
    2.) Greened potatoes
    3.) Tomato leaves

WEEDS

The term "weed" is relative. It's been said that "weeds" are just plants that we haven't found a use for yet. Dandelions, for example, are weeds to some people. But other people consider them a delicacy, and gather the tender spring or fall leaves and fry them in an oil and vinegar sauce, mixed with several spices, for a "wet salad." Others pick the blossoms and make a tasty wine.

"Weeds" have become a negative symbol for modern gardeners. Somehow, weeds in a person's garden have become equated with "dust" in their house. Modern gardeners have made a fetish of clearing all weeds from their gardens.

What's wrong with weeds? Three major things, so it is said: They rob your plants of sunlight; they extract valuable nutrients from your soil; and their root structure prevents moisture from reaching your plants.

All of this is true, but only relatively true. For example, if you live in a hot section of the country, some of the plants in your garden don't welcome so much sun, and weeds can help shade them.

Weeds can extract nutrients from your soil — if the weeds are excessive. But a sprinkling of weeds isn't going to bother your plants. Like all living entities, your plants will seem to enjoy the competition. Next time you're driving in the country and pass a field of corn or other vegetable crop, stop and get out to examine the rows from up close. Although the areas between the rows are relatively free of weeds, the areas between the plants do have weeds growing in them. If professional gardeners can excuse some weeds, so can you.

As for weeds robbing moisture from your plants, that's a negligible problem. Some seasons will be extremely wet, and you'll be glad there are weeds around to keep your plants from drowning. If it's too dry, then you'll be watering your plants (and weeds) anyway.

Another aspect of weeds you will want to consider is this: If weeds are growing next to your crops, they can serve as extra hosts for the variety of bugs that will visit your garden. There are only so many bugs to a given garden area. If they are chewing on your weeds, then that much less will they be chewing on your plants. Of course some bugs have specialties, as I mentioned earlier in this section.

Some very friendly weeds

Whether your first garden is a small patch, or extensive, you are going to find the same weeds popping up in it. You might want to make use of some of them. There are eight major useful plants (we can't call them weeds anymore) that can be beneficial around your household. By using them, you will

be adding eight more plants automatically to your produce
list.

I have talked to "experts" who have been gardening for
years, yet they have automatically destroyed these plants
year after year. By being cognizant of their usefulness you'll
be a few jumps ahead of some of the pros.

Here are the "Big Eight":

Lamb's-quarters (Chenopodium album) — This one is pro-
lific. It's the "sparrow" of the weed world and should be one
you should get to know first.

As with most plants, the young tender leaves in spring, or
the tops of the plants (which are the new leaves) are the tastiest.

Lamb's-quarters is also known by these country names:
Pigweed (Canada), white goosefoot, and dirty dick.

The leaves are oval, wedge-shaped, with wavy teeth. If
left to grow, the plants reach three to five feet in height.

Lamb's-quarters will pop up in your garden earlier than
your lettuce. Gather the leaves, break them up into smaller
pieces and wash. Serve with your favorite dressing for a tasty
(and nutritious) salad. It is also an excellent substitute for
spinach.

In New Mexico and Arizona, the Indians gather the
young and tender plants and boil them as pot herbs, alone or
with other food.

Common Mallow (Valva species) — This one is sometimes
called "creeping Charlie," or low mallow, or cheese plant
(*Malva* rotundifolia). The leaves are round and heart-shaped,
about an inch across, depending how mature the plant is.
They are dark green and edged with rounded teeth.

When you pull it from your garden, you'll recognize common mallow by its long root that goes several inches straight
down. When you pull the plant, pull off the buds too, which
appear all summer long. They can be eaten raw in your salads, or give body to your summer soups. Also, if you find
enough of them, try cooking them like Brussels sprouts and

serve with salt and butter. (Okra, incidentally, is of the mallow family.)

Purslane (Portulacca oleracea) — Purslane is a succulent, tropical-looking plant that grows as a flat, spreading vine, close to the ground. The flowers are small and yellow and bloom in the middle of summer, but only around noon. It is also known as pigweed or pussley. (Incidentally, several garden weeds are known as "pigweed.")

The young leaves are excellent to add to salads, and the older ones can be added to your soups, cooked like spinach or even pickled in salt and vinegar.

Common Plantain (Plantago major) — You'll recognize this plant best in late summer when it sends up a five-inch spike with seeds on it. Kids like to pull these spikes off and run their fingers down the stem, causing the seeds to fly off.

Don't confuse this name with the plantain of Central and South America — the baking or frying banana.

Plantain is sometimes called snakeweed, ripple grass or waybread. The young, early leaves of this plant can be used as a salad herb or cooked like spinach, but plantain is best known as an herbal remedy. To quote from Ben Charles Harris's *The Compleat Herbal* (Barre, 1972):

"Plantain is an excellent vulnerary and astringent for external applications, to draw forth and remove felons and splinters, and to poultice boils and bruises. For recent insect bites, sores, and indolent ulcers, the leaves need only be crushed and dipped in hot water and applied to the affected area."

When I was a kid, my mother would tape a plantain leaf to any bruises, boils, or hard-to-get-out splinters I happened to be sporting. Ma Nordstrum's dog bruised his leg when a log fell on it the other day. She told me she Scotch-taped a plantain leaf to Rusty's leg and it healed in no time. Plantain: the versatile remedy for man or beast.

Curly Dock (Rumex crispus) — Curly dock probably has

the deepest roots of any of the garden weeds. In fact, unless
it's been a wet week, when you pull the plant, the root will
probably break off. But why pull it?

It is also known as yellow dock and narrow dock. In any
case, you'll recognize it by its large, curled leaves.

Curly dock is rich in vitamin A (almost twice as much as
spinach; see page 104) and many other nutrients.

Green Amaranth (Amaranthus retroflexus) — You'll recognize it by its bright red root. But again, why pull it? It is
probably more nutritious, ounce for ounce, than any of the
other vegetables growing in your garden. You can increase
the size of your next boiled-greens dish by tossing in the available amaranth (and other garden weeds) from your garden.

Stinging Nettle (Urtica dioica) — This is not a pleasant
plant to contemplate, especially if you are allergic to its toxic
oils — they sting! But having nettles in your garden is a compliment; they grow only in rich soil.

The nettle is from the mint family which you will recognize by its stem. All plants of the mint family have a square
stem. The leaves are opposite from each other, heart-shaped,
finely toothed on the margins, and tapering to points. Nettles
are highly nutritious and delicious. They must be gathered in
early spring (with gloves) and cooked like spinach. Cooking
destroys the sting. Incidentally, if you get stung, roll some
nearby curly dock in a ball and rub it on. It helps! You can also
make an excellent tea from nettles. Hang a bunch up in a dry
place for three weeks, then run them through a collander. Put
your tea in a jar with a lid and use as you would regular tea.
Delicious.

Dandelion (Taraxacum officinale) — Of all these "weeds,"
the dandelion will probably be the most recognizable to you.
But you must learn to recognize it before the flowers appear,
because after it has blossomed, the leaves are no longer tender for eating.

The most popular way to serve young dandelion leaves is

to sauté them in oil or bacon grease mixed with salt and pepper and a few herbs of your choice. But here are a couple of recipes:

DANDELION GREENS

After washing thoroughly, cook in boiling water 5 minutes. Drain and throw away water, and put greens into another pot of boiling water with salt. Cook 10 minutes. Drain and chop fine; add butter and a little cream and serve with chopped hard-boiled egg.

ESCALLOPED DANDELION GREENS

2 qts. dandelion greens	1 beef bouillon cube
1 cup water	¼ cup grated cheese
¼ tsp. salt	¼ cup buttered bread
2 tbs. butter	crumbs
1½ tbs. flour	Pepper
2 cups hot milk	Paprika

Cut off the roots and imperfect leaves from young, tender dandelions. Wash thoroughly and separate the leaves. Cook until tender, about 25 to 30 minutes, removing cover after 10 minutes. Drain, add seasoning, and chop fine. Melt butter in top of double boiler, blend in flour, and add milk in which bouillon cube has been dissolved, stirring constantly. Place cooked dandelions in a greased casserole, cover with the white sauce, and spread over top grated cheese which has been combined with the bread crumbs. Bake in a moderate oven (350° F.) about 20 minutes or until top is well browned.

These plants have a threefold benefit: They're plentiful, free, and highly nutritious.

The authoritative "Composition of Foods," published by the U.S. Department of Agriculture and recently updated, includes five of the above eight "weeds" in its comprehensive analysis of foods. Here is a breakdown which will allow you to compare them to lettuce and spinach.

GARDEN VEGETABLE	Water %	Food Energy Calories/100 g.	Protein g/100 g.	Fat — g/100 g.	Carbo-hydrate Total	Carbo-hydrate Fiber g/100 g.	Ash g/100 g.	Calcium: mg/100 g.	Phosphorus mg/100 g.	Iron mg/100 g.	Sodium mg/100 g.	Potassium mg/100 g.	Vitamin A: I.U./100 g.	Thiamine mg/100 g.	Riboflavin gm/100 g.	Niacin mg/100 g.	Vitamin C: mg/100 g.
(Head Lettuce) Iceberg Lettuce	95.5	13	0.9	.1	2.9	.5	.6	20	22	.5	9	175	330	.06	.06	.3	6
Spinach	90.7	26	3.2	.3	4.3	.6	1.5	93	51	3.1	71	470	8,100	.10	.20	.6	51
GARDEN "WEED"																	
Lambs Quarters	84.3	43	4.2	.8	7.3	2.1	3.4	309	72	1.2			11,600	.16	.44	1.2	80
Purslane	92.5	21	1.7	.4	3.8	.9	1.6	103	39	3.5			2,500	.03	.10	.5	25
Curly Dock	90.9	28	2.1	.3	5.6	.8	1.1	66	41	1.6	5	338	12,900	.09	.09	.5	119
Green Amaranth	86.9	36	3.5	.5	6.5	1.3	2.6	267	67	3.9		411	6,100	.08	.16	1.4	80
(Greens) Dandelion	85.6	45	2.7	.7	9.2	1.6	1.8	187	66	3.1	76	397	14,000	.19	.26	.5	35

COMPOSITION OF FOODS, 100 GRAMS, EDIBLE PORTION.

Credit: U.S. Department of Agriculture.

If you would like to pursue the subject of "garden weeds" further (there are many other uses for these eight plants that have been known for centuries) I would recommend the following:

The Book of Herb Cookery
Irene Botsford Hoffman
Houghton-Mifflin Company

Stalking the Healthful Herbs
Euell Gibbons
David Mckay Company

The Healing Power of Herbs
May Bethel
Wilshire Book Company

A Modern Herbal (Two Volumes)
Mrs. M. Grieve
Hafner Publishing Company

The Compleat Herbal
Ben Charles Harris
Barre Publishing Company

The pleasant and advantageous aspect of these free garden plants, is that once you begin to recognize them you'll find that they grow not only in your garden, but in vacant lots, fields, country roadsides and along stream banks. Gathering them offers a good excuse for a family outing!

Poisonous Weeds
Probably the greatest deterrent to most gardeners using plants other than what they have planted by seed is the fear that the plant may be poisonous.

If you have positively identified the eight friendly plants above (and identification is simple because they have no similar-looking cousins which might be poisonous), then you're safe in gathering them for use.

PLANTING INDOORS

To keep indoor planting *really* simple, I suggest you invest in the do-it-yourself indoor-starter kits that are usually found on the shelves of supermarkets in early spring. These commercial kits feature all the popular garden vegetables and it's almost impossible to make a mistake with them. The directions are explicit and the results are worth the tinkering time you put to them.

If you'd like to be a little more flexible, try planting seeds indoors.

First of all, keep in mind that you are attempting to duplicate outdoor conditions two to three weeks ahead of the time you plant your seeds. Those weather conditions are basically 60 to 70 degrees in temperature, sunny, and generally moist. (Slow germinating seeds take longer. The information on the seed packet will indicate when you should start your seeds indoors.)

Buy "flats" from the seed catalog or at your garden store and fill them with equal parts of mixed sand, compost, and black soil. To assure there are no microorganisms in the mixture that might affect your plants, bake the mixture in a pan in your oven for an hour at 400 degrees. When the soil cools off, plant your seeds in rows, much as you would in the garden, except the distance between the rows can be closer.

Set your flats near a sunny window in a cool location of your house. Avoid any drafts. Continue to duplicate nature by keeping the soil damp — but not too damp. If you're forgetful, you can give your seeds a good watering and then cover the flats with a piece of clear plastic, which will keep the moisture intact. You won't have to water again 'til your seedlings start appearing.

As soon as they do appear, start thinning them out with a pair of tweezers to an inch apart. Give them room!

If you've timed it right, your seedlings will be just the right size to transplant into your garden at the right time. The hardy ones will go in early, the not-so-hardy will wait 'til later — but they won't have been planted 'til later.

When seedlings are transplanted, they experience what gardeners call "shock." That is, they wilt, appear to be sick, and don't look very perky. The younger the plant is when it is transplanted, the less shock it seems to experience. For this reason, gardeners like to transplant twice, once from the original flat into a second flat where they'll have more leg room, and then after a week or two into the garden.

Removing seedlings from a flat.

Transplant into a new flat, 2 inches apart.

Make the first transplanting when the seedlings have their first two *true* leaves. These will be the third and fourth leaves appearing on your seedling. If you don't plan on making this intermediate transplanting, let your seedlings grow a little larger and then make the transition.

Gardeners have found that it's nearly impossible to make the house-to-garden transition in one day without a catastrophe. The sudden change of environment is too drastic. They have learned it's better to accustom their seedlings to the outdoors, a little at a time, much as you would an infant. If it's a pleasant day, place your flat(s) outdoors in a sheltered area for a few hours. Increase the time, and in two weeks, you plants should be adjusted. Of course, if the temperature drops, or heavy winds hit the area, keep the plants inside. This whole technique is called "hardening off."

Not all of your transplants will survive the move to the garden, so transplant more than you anticipate needing, and then thin the extras out in a couple of weeks.

You'd be a rare gardener indeed, if you had 100% success on your indoor plantings the first time. It's really difficult to duplicate, indoors, the environment your plants will be introduced to outdoors. But to bring you close to that 100% here are some points:

a) *Damping Off.* Your seedling will look sickly from this fungus disease. You can help prevent "damping off" by providing the kind of healthy soil described above. And don't over-water your plants.

b) *Spindly Plants* result when your seedlings are overcrowded or they must reach a long distance for sunlight, or your soil is too warm or too wet. Your soil should be cool — especially at night. Tender seedlings (cucumbers, tomatoes, melons, etc.) require a night temperature not over 65 degrees F. Hardy seedlings (cabbage, lettuce, etc.) require not more than 55 degrees F.

c) *Bent Stems* come from overcrowding and uneven exposure to the light source. Turn your flat each day and the seedlings will grow straight. If a natural light source isn't available to you, ask your florist or nursery man about fluorescent lighting that's designed for houseplants.

TRANSPLANTING

Transplanting is foreign to nature. Plants aren't prepared

for it and consequently don't adjust to it as well as the rest of us living beings on this planet.

If you have to transplant, take as much soil as you can with the roots. Seedlings from a flat, of course, have a less extensive root system than, say, a five-inch-high cabbage plant in your garden. It stands to reason that if you transplant with a trowel, you're hardly going to transfer as much soil as if you use a garden spade. Be sure, of course, you have dug a hole equally as large for your transplanted plant to fit in.

Your home-grown seedling is ready to transfer into the garden.

Much of the harm from transplanting comes when the plant's roots are exposed to the air and allowed to dry out. When you make the transfer, use a lot of water before and after. The damp soil has a tendency to help the soil seal itself together and not allow the drying effect of air to reach the roots of the newly transferred plant.

THE HERB GARDEN

Walk out your back door, pick a few sprigs of spearmint

and you can serve your guests a zestful tea. Or you might want to serve them tea made from sweet fennel, bergamot, or camomile.

At lunch time, enhance the flavor of your soup du jour with some home-grown thyme and coriander.

For supper, add some anise and tarragon seeds to your salad, some basil in your ground chuck, and dill and chives in the sauce.

For breakfast, sprinkle some home-grown sage in your egg and cheese soufflé.

A general rule for growing herbs is grow them in full sunlight and poor soil (that's a switch!). Another rule I would like to suggest is grow them near the back door, where they'll be handy when they're needed.

Herbs are often available as plants at the nursery, and are always available in seed packets. Directions for planting always come with the seed packets and the supermarket starter kits. But one thing the directions don't usually include is when to harvest your herbs.

Here's a brief run-down on when to harvest some of the more popular herbs:

Harvest the seeds when they begin to turn brown: anise, coriander, dill, fennel, and nasturtium.

Harvest the young leaves, and dry them: bergamot, chervil, parsley, rose geranium.

Harvest the tips when they're beginning to bloom, and dry them: basil, fennel, lavender, sage, spearmint, tansy, tarragon.

Harvest the tips in full bloom and dry them: lavender, rosemary, and thyme.

Drying herbs can be done several ways. Hang them in bunches in a shed, out of the sunlight, and where they'll get some air circulation.

Or, make a net bag, (a mesh wedding veil is excellent material), drop your flowers, buds, or leaves into the bag and hang it in the kitchen.

Or, put your herbs on a cookie tray and put in the oven at low heat for several hours.

Or, if you really want to control the drying process, (you might want to try dehydrating some of your garden produce this way too...) look into a dehydrator, such as the Equi-Flow (514 State Ave., Marysville, Washington, 98270).

Here are two books that give details on how to grow herbs:

The Concise Herbal Encyclopedia
Donald Law
St. Martin's Press

Better Health with Culinary Herbs
Ben Charles Harris
Barre Publishing Company

●

Hardy plants aren't bothered by the frost, but tender plants are. Here is a list of hardy plants. You can plant them very early in the spring, providing the soil isn't too wet: (These are also listed in order as to which can be planted the earliest): peas, spinach, lettuce, potatoes, onions, leeks, beets, broccoli, and cabbage. The first three, you might even try to plant the previous fall.

Tender plants don't like the frost (it kills them). Check the map for the date you can probably expect the last spring frost before planting any of these tender plants: cauliflower, peppers, tomatoes, cucumbers, squash, pumpkins, and beans. Mother Nature often visits with an unexpected late frost, but then again sometimes she doesn't. If the weather report calls for a late spring frost and your tender plants have sprouted above ground already, protect them with newspapers, cardboard boxes, etc. If they're still in the germinating stage (below ground) — no harm will be done by the frost.

WHEN CAN I START PLANTING?

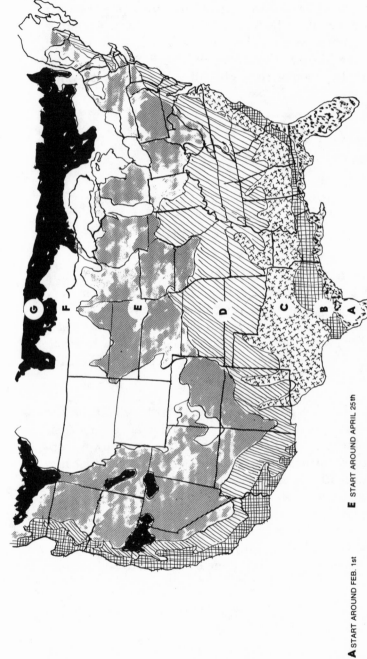

A START AROUND FEB. 1st

B START AROUND THE MIDDLE OF FEBRUARY

C START AROUND MARCH 10th

D START AROUND APRIL 1st

E START AROUND APRIL 25th

F START AROUND JUNE 1st

G START AROUND JUNE 10th

VEG.	WHEN TO PLANT SEED LONGEVITY	HOW FAR APART? HOW DEEP?	ROWS APART	FAMILY OTHER FAMILY MEMBERS	SEEDLINGS	MATURITY
ASPARAGUS	Early spring Plant roots immediately	18"	5'	Liliaceae		2 years
BEAN (Snap)	After danger of frost 3 years	4"	2½'	Leguminosae		75-90 days
BEET	Very early spring 4 years	3"	18"	Chenopodiaceae Swiss chard Spinach		50-60 days
BROCCOLI	Very early spring 3 years	18"	2½'	Cruciferae Cabbage Cauliflower Mustard		80 days
BRUSSELS SPROUTS	Very early spring 3 years	18"	3'	Cruciferae Broccoli Cabbage Cauliflower Mustard Kale		100 days
CABBAGE	Very early spring 4 years	18"	2½'	Cruciferae Mustard Cabbage Kale Radish Turnip		65-120 days
CARROT	Early spring 3 years	2"	1½'	Umbelliferae Celery Parsnip		70-75 days

VEG.	WHEN TO PLANT SEED LONGEVITY	HOW FAR APART? HOW DEEP?	ROWS APART	FAMILY OTHER FAMILY MEMBERS	SEEDLINGS	MATURITY
CANTALOUPE	After danger of frost / 5 years	5' / 1½"	5'	Cucurbitaceae / Gourds Cucumber Squash Pumpkin		75-100 days
CAULIFLOWER	Early spring / 4 years	1½' / ½"	2½'	Cruciferae / Broccoli Mustard Cabbage Kale		90-95 days
CELERY	Plant indoors 10 weeks before final frost / 3 years	6" / 1" (TRANSPLANTS)	24"	Umbelliferae / Carrot Parsnip		5 months
CORN	Early spring / 3 years	15" / 1"	2½'	Graminae / Grass		80-90 days
CUCUMBER	After danger of frost / 5 years	5' / 1½"	6'	Cucurbitaceae / Gourd Cantaloupe Squash Pumpkin		70-75 days
GARLIC	Very early spring / 1 year	4" / 2"	2'	Liliaceae / Asparagus Lily Leek Onion		90 days
KOHLRABI	Very early spring / 4 years	6" / ½"	18"	Cruciferae / Mustard Cabbage Cauliflower Kale		55-65 days

VEG.	WHEN TO PLANT SEED LONGEVITY	HOW FAR APART? HOW DEEP?	ROWS APART	FAMILY OTHER FAMILY MEMBERS	SEEDLINGS	MATURITY
LEEK	Very early spring 1 year	6" 6" (plants)	1½'	Liliaceae Asparagus Lily Onion Garlic		85-130 days
LETTUCE	Very early spring 6 years	10" ¼"	1½'	Lactuca sativa		45-85 days
LIMA BEAN	Spring 4 years	6" 1½"	30"	Leguminosae Pea Bean		65-75 days
OKRA	Spring 4 years	15" 1½"	3'	Malvaceae Mallow Hibiscus		55-65 days
ONION	Very early spring 1 year	4" 1½"	1½'	Liliaceae Asparagus Lily Leek Garlic		120 days
PARSNIP	Early spring 1 year	3" 1½"	1½'	Umbelliferae Carrot Celery		120 days
PEA	Very early spring 3 years	2" 2"	3'	Leguminosae Bean		65-80 days

VEG.	WHEN TO PLANT SEED LONGEVITY	HOW FAR APART? HOW DEEP?	ROWS APART	FAMILY OTHER FAMILY MEMBERS	SEEDLINGS	MATURITY
PEPPER	After last frost — 2 years	2' — ½"	3'	Solanaceae — Potato Tomato Tobacco Petunia		115 days
POTATO	Early spring — 8 months	1' — 4"	2'	Solanaceae — Eggplant Tomato Pepper Tobacco Petunia		100-120 days
PUMPKIN	Spring — 4 years	5' — 1"	5'	Cucurbitaceae — Squash Gourd Cucumber Cantaloupe		65-75 days
RADISH	Early spring — 4 years	½" — ½"	6"	Cruciferae — Mustard Cabbage Kale Broccoli Cauliflower		25-60 days
RHUBARB	90 days before first freeze — Perennial	3' — 2"	4'	Polygonaceae — Buckwheat		12 months
RUTABAGA	90 days before first freeze — 4 years	4" — ½"	1½'	Cruciferae — Turnip Cabbage Kohlrabi Broccoli		90 days
SPINACH	Very early spring — 3 years	3" — 1½"	12"	Chenopodiaceae — Beet Swiss chard		40-70 days

VEG.	WHEN TO PLANT SEED LONGEVITY	HOW FAR APART? HOW DEEP?	ROWS APART	FAMILY OTHER FAMILY MEMBERS	SEEDLINGS	MATURITY
SQUASH	Early spring 4 years	5' ½'	6'	Cucurbitaceae Pumpkin Cushaw Gourd Cucumber Cantaloupe		Summer 55 days Winter 150 days
SWISS CHARD	Very early spring 3 years	10" 1"	18"	Chenopodiaceae Beet Spinach		55 days
TOMATO	(Plants): After last frost 4 years	3' PLANTS: 1" BELOW FORMER LEVEL	4'	Solanaceae Potato Tobacco Eggplant Pepper		(Seed) 115 days
TURNIP	Spring 4 years	3" ½"	1½'	Cruciferae Rutabaga Cabbage Kohlrabi Broccoli		65 days
WATERMELON	After last frost 2 years	8' 1"	8'	Cucurbitaceae Cucumber Gourd Cantaloupe Squash		85 days

POST SCRIPT

A fellow gardener just came into my office and asked, "Did you ever write that book on gardening you said you were going to write?"

I replied that I had and that at any moment the book would be on sale across the nation. He said, "I gotta get me one of them!"

"But you're an experienced gardener...." I said. "What could you learn from a *simple* garden book?"

"I gotta fill in the blanks....with some of that basic stuff," he said, "the stuff I either forgot, or never did learn in the beginning!"

It's nice to know you're ahead of some of the experienced gardeners at this point—and it's nice to know you did it by gliding through the garden, skipping over the non-essentials as you went.

Now the time has come to fill in some more blanks. The basic training is over. The learning from this point on comes as you start flying by the seat-of-the-pants. Some of it will come from trial and error, a lot from the veteran garden friends you'll acquire. And you might start filling in the blanks with some information from those complicated garden tomes you once thought too technical and dry. They just might come alive and start speaking your language.

Now that you're off and flying, and the experimental world of gardening unfolds before you, many new doors will be opening. You'll be discovering new insights, many of which you'll want to share with fellow gardeners—like the veteran who wanted to go back to basics and learn from this book, or the fellow who wrote this book, me, I'll be there, too, eager to borrow and to learn from your garden discoveries.

GLOSSARY

Aerobic Composting — If your compost materials are exposed to air, they will decompose (ferment) with the aid of airborne bacteria.

Anaerobic Composting — When you cover your compost pile, say, with a large sheet of plastic, the compost is decomposed by bacteria that exists in the absence of air.

Blight — If many of your plant leaves are turning brown, they no doubt are diseased and are being attacked by disease-carrying organisms. There are several such diseases that fall into the category commonly referred to as "blight."

Clay — Soil is ordinarily composed of a mixture of clay, silt, sand, and organic matter. The combination is called loam. Clay particles are fine and tend to compact, making it difficult for air to reach plant roots, and for the gardener to cultivate. Pure clay won't produce many crops.

Cold Frame — A frame in which you put your seedlings. It's higher in the back and lower in the front so it can catch sunlight. The top is a glass or plastic (clear) cover which can be raised or lowered, depending on the temperature.

Compost — Just about anything that is bio-degradable is eligible as compost. Pieces of wood, though, ought to be shredded, to make their decomposition speedier. Providing there's a reasonable balance of nutrients, compost is the most complete fertilizer for your garden.

Cross-Pollination — The breeze in your garden usually does the job for you by transferring the pollen from one flower to the stigma of another.

Cultivation — This is what happens when you keep weeds from growing in your garden.

Damping Off — Often happens to young seedlings that you have planted indoors. Caused by a fungus. Seedling becomes infected at base of plant and dies.

Earthworms — These are silent workers in your garden. The traffic in the subsoil helps to aerate your garden. Their excretions (castings) help to fertilize. Their dead bodies also serve as fertilizer. They don't co-exist with toxic chemical sprays, so you have to choose one or the other.

Fungus — from the family of mushrooms, molds, mildews, rusts, and smuts. They're called helpful in the garden when they serve to decompose dead vegetation. They're not helpful when they disfigure or kill your living crops.

Germination — happens when a seed comes to life and starts producing leaves and roots of its own. Some seeds have long life and will germinate even after four or five years. Some can't be kept more than a year.

Green Manure — The roots from certain plants and grasses penetrate deep into the soil. When they decay, they add important fertilizer to your garden soil.

Hardening Off — The seedlings you've planted indoors in the early spring have to be introduced to the outside world gradually, otherwise they won't adjust well to their new garden environment. The process of exposing your seedlings gradually to the outdoors (placing the flats outdoors for an increasing time each day) is called "hardening off."

Heaving — occurs in winter and spring when there are alternate periods of thawing and freezing. Moisture seeps into fissures in the soil, then freezes, causing the soil to expand (heave). When the soil thaws again, plant roots are exposed. When the next freeze comes, plant roots are killed, if they can't take it.

Hot Bed — The same thing as a cold except that some sort of artificial heat (heating cable) or natural heat (fresh manure) keeps the seedlings warm.

Humus — organic matter in an advanced state of decomposition.

Leaching — When it rains, or when you water your garden, a certain amount of nutrients are carried away from your garden to wherever the H_2O goes. That could be straight through (to the water table below) or it could run off the surface, into a ditch, and eventually make its way to a creek, river, ocean, etc. Therefore, excessive water can be harmful to your garden, especially if you're not in the practice of adding healthy amounts of compost, and other nutrients to it annually.

Loam — A friable mixture of silt, clay, sand, and organic matter.

Mulch — A layer of organic material placed over bare soil in the garden. It helps to retain moisture in the soil, hold down weed growth, and, when it decomposes, it adds to the fertility of the soil. Gardeners usually prefer hay as their mulch, but many gardeners use pine needles, sawdust, leaves, or a combination of any of these.

Pollination — When a mass of tiny spores float through the air and one lands on the stigma of the same plant variety, a new seed-producing fruit is begun. The pollen can get there several ways: wind, gravity, insects, birds, or artificially.

Pruning — The process of trimming out part of a plant (it may be a healthy part or diseased), in order that the original plant might benefit in some way.

Root Crops — These are the vegetables we cultivate more for what they produce underground than above.

Rotation — Plants give and take from your soil. Rotation of your vegetable varieties means to change the location of vegetables each season to assure a good soil balance. Rotation also discourages garden pests from settling into one section of your garden and finding the same meal each year.

Soil Testing — In large acreage, soil testing proves valuable. If tests show there is a general overall deficiency, some adjustments can be made. In the home garden, any deficiencies are generally corrected through the use of composts or the introduction of an all-purpose chemical fertilizer. In the case where certain plants aren't thriving, as when peppers are producing abundant leaves and no fruit, the cause can be traced to individual needs of the plant rather than a general deficiency of the soil. These needs can usually be met without going through the process of elaborate soil testing.

Thinning — Planting more seeds than necessary in case some of the seeds don't sprout. Once the seedlings are up, you "thin" or eliminate the excess. These thinned seedlings can be transplanted somewhere else, used in salads, or put into the compost heap. Removing buds on your vine crops is a form of thinning and is mentioned in the section on pruning (page 41).

INDEX

A

Acid soil 83
Acorn squash 64, 66
Aerobic composting **121**
Alkaline 23
Allergic reaction 102
Almanac 43
Anise 110
Aluminum foil 79
Amaranth, green 69, 102, 104
Anaerobic 47, **121**
Aphid 93, 94
Appetizer 83
Artichokes, Jerusalem 56
Ashes, wood 23, 29, 34, 48, 56, 91
Asparagus 43, 49, **76**, **113**
Auxiliary buds 28

B

Badminton racket 23, 51, 92
Baked beans 36, 37
Banana, plantain 101
Basil 110
Beans 7, 13, 14, **36**, 38, 43, **56**, 69, 75, **77**, **113**
Bean, lima 36, **77**
Bees, pollination 33
Beetle, cucumber 34, 93
Beetle, Japanese 93, 94
Beets 44, 50, **53**, 54, **113**
Beginner 4
Bell pepper 55
Bergamot 110
Bibb lettuce 17
Bibliography 105, 111
Birds 92, 94, 97
Blanching 79, 84
Blender 79, 95
Blight 37, **121**
Blossoms, see: flowers
Bluebird 94
Bolt, going to seed 42, 52, 69
Bone meal 56
Book of Herb Cookery 105
Borsch 53

Broccoli 4, 42, 43, **50**, 52, 78, 91, 97, **113**
Brussel sprouts 4, 13, 43, **77**, 91, 97, **113**
Buds, auxiliary 28
Bugs, see: insects
Bulbs 41, 44, 97
Bulbs, onion 21
Burlap 31
Bush bean 13, **36**, 56, 77
Buttercup squash 65
Butterfly, cabbage worm 23, 79, 92
Butterhead lettuce 17
Butternut squash 65, 66

C

Cabbage 7, 13, 15, **22**, 44, 51, 77, 79, 83, 91, 97, 108, **113**
Cabbage salad, frozen 24
Canning 49
Cantaloupe 71, **72**, 92, **114**
Carrot 7, 13, **19**, 20, 22, 39, 40, 44, 50, 81, **113**
Casserole, zucchini 64
Castor bean 97
Cat 55, 92
Catalog 63
Cauliflower 42, 44, 51, **79**, 91, 97, **114**
Celeriac 81
Celery 44, **80**, **114**
Cellar, root, see: storage, winter
Chamomile 110
Chantenay carrot 19
Cheesecloth 17
Chemical sprays **95**
Cherry tomato 25
Chervil 110
Chickadee 94
Chicken 55, 94
Chinese lantern 97
Chives 110
Clay 11, 32, **121**

NOTES

NOTES